QUESTS

QUESTS

David M. Burns

Writers Club Press
San Jose   New York   Lincoln   Shanghai

QUESTS

Writers Club Press
an imprint of iUniverse, Inc.

For information address:
iUniverse, Inc.
5220 S. 16th St., Suite 200
Lincoln, NE 68512
www.iuniverse.com

Book is mainly non-fiction, but contains four chapters describing imaginary ancestors.

ISBN: 0-595-21175-5

Printed in the United States of America

DECEMBER 1, 1928–

◆

First, I hope you'll kindly forgive that over-the-top cover photo, shutter snapped courtesy of my beloved wife, Sandy. Cover was the only chance to get some visible color into this *Mss*. At the time it seemed like a good idea to throw in the brightest hues possible. But as I so often do, I'm afraid I overdid it. This seems, now that I look at it, maybe *too much…FAR* too much. Sorry!

The background shows wisteria climbing up the walls surrounding our backyard at 1712 19th Street NW, Washington, DC. The block of coal is from Straight Creek in Bell County, Kentucky, and you will soon understand why I had to include it. The orange jacket and wild shades are a bow to old friends in Princeton's Class of 1953, and a reminder of four happy years in what really IS, on mature reflection, 'The Best Old Place Of All.'

The beret looks a little squirrelly, but I was seriously concerned that my baldhead might reflect so much sun the photo would be over-exposed. For those that like to adorn the old cranial globe with such pie-plates, may I add a plug? The one you see is from Gorostiaga, an absolutely marvelous shop at Victor No. 9, in the heart of the Old Quarter of Bilbao, Spain. Like all Basque *boinas*, it's about 20% bigger than the effete, inadequate models affected by the French.

If you have sharp eyes, you might possibly make out a vaguely equine animal adorning the tie. If you happen to be a Republican, may

1

I dissemble and aver, 'No, this is *not* the donkey of The Democratic Party.' Since much of what follows takes place in the coalfields of Southeastern Kentucky, let's assume it is a reminder of the thousands of unfortunate ponies, mules, and jackasses that spent their *entire lives* pulling heavy coal cars out of the pitch-black insides of The Cumberland Mountains, dumping coal into tipples and shakers, and thence into the tiny hands of grimy slate-pickers, boys too young to go inside the mines. I pity the ponies, asses and mules, and I pity also the thousands of two-legged workers, many my distant kinfolk, that had to make it from '*The Portal*' up to the face of the seam, and LOAD '*Sixteen Tons*'!

Anyway, Thanks! for reading this. This book is intended for myself, for my wife, Sandy, and for our two fine sons, David and his kids Connor, Meghan and Kady, and Patrick and Carolyn and their kids Sarah and Austin. It's mainly a record…'*Back Up The File*,' as computer gurus constantly exhort us, just in case senility, certainly senescence, one or both tapping faintly at the door?, causes me to go gaga, wafting all memory out my ears, blown Who Knows Where? *Gone With The Wind*!

But perhaps you may actually find it interesting?! *Wow!* For me, that would be simply WONDERFUL!

*   *   *   *   *

I tap on the QuietKey keyboard of my Dell Dimension 4300, dispatching electrons through nano circuits and layered silicon of Pentium IV and 512 kilobyte RAM chips. Ubiquitous, ever-helpful MicroSoft [via WORD] encodes the text, which is then stored for retrieval or alteration via magnetization of iron oxide. An image of the words is displayed on my 19-inch Princeton-brand flat monitor, which also continuously irradiates my eyeballs and brain. In these and other tasks, I am abetted by a do-it-all Xerox Work Center M950 copier/scanner/printer, Panasonic KX-TS20-W Integrated 2-line Telephone System, and Sony

ICF-2010 world band radio. I am linked…in fact TIGHTLY BOUND…via 56k modem and *starpower.net* to Websites around the world, and via e-mail to friends and family.

STAR POWER indeed! Like you and every living thing, I am congealed stardust. The words I write stride continents and bounce off satellites. I zip, I fly! My e-mails race at light speed through fiber optic cable. The Web delivers close-up views of galaxies, and the four-letter cryptogram of the double helix, the code for every living thing that rides with us on this blue marble, racing through the black void of space. I have VAST resources at my tips, more information…at least more words [regrettably, not more wisdom!]…than ALL books in ALL libraries—*ever*.

In short…JUST LIKE YOU…I've got some Jim-dandy tools here. I also have time. But…Do I Have Anything To Say? **WHY** did you have to ask that question? Why **THAT** question?! What can I possibly write of interest to you…or EVEN TO ME?

The experts say: write what you know. Well, what I know, or think I know, is mainly myself, or at least the bits and pieces of my life I am able to remember, or permit myself to remember, which is of course the merest fraction of what happened. Electronic tools NOT effective, '*star power*' of ZERO help, regarding the terror and drama, a near-murder, on a Saturday night sixty-eight years ago in a rented house in a small town in Kentucky. No Website for that one! NO WAY to download ANYTHING! *Nada.*

Like the phalanx of Scots policemen trudging head down, shoulder-to-shoulder through shards of metal and flesh littering the debris field of Lockerbie, I also trudge…not through Lockerbie, but through the debris field of Memories. I hope I am as sharp-eyed as the Scots. I will retrieve every likely bit I see. I will assemble the bits as meticulously as I can. Perhaps I can fit together a simulacrum of a PORTION of what, maybe, perhaps, actually happened. I will understand the assemblage—if I can. And I will report.

THE REPORT (you are reading it now) will be as clear as I can make it.

A Message:

  FROM: The Past.

    TO: The Present.

      FOR: Me, my wife, sons, and grandkids.

        Cc: To YOU!

How to begin, what to say? Well, I will do my best to avoid inventing stuff to fill in the gaps, some as wide and as deep as Western canyons, and many quite significant. And I will TRY [I say 'try'...no guarantees here, *caveat emptor*!]...I will try to be honest. But given a lifetime of self-delusion, flight, avoidance of every kind, self-deception, outright dishonesty, rationalization, dissembling, justification...HOW do you do this? Do you suddenly wake up...and SHAZAM! there you are: *HONEST!?*

Friends of Bill...and You Know Who You Are!...say 'You're only as sick as your secrets.' Let's get serious here: Are you saying: If I tell it ALL, THIS will generate 'mental health'? Solid brain? *Mens sana*? Dynamite personality? Pardon me, but I don't believe it!

ALL? *ALL!* (Well, I can censor myself later...)

Does the possible result justify the time and energy required? I lived such-and-such a span. I experienced this-and-that. So? What's your point? Age 73, excellent health, some synapses damaged beyond repair by alcohol, but, surprisingly, despite abuse, brain more or less intact:

Therefore, as The Learned Rabbi said:

  If not me, WHO?

    If not now, WHEN?

      And furthermore, WHY NOT?

    *   *   *   *   *

I was born December 1, 1928 in Pineville, Kentucky, a little town about twelve miles north of Cumberland Gap. The 'hospital' was a two-story frame structure, The Old Gragg House, at the end of Cherry Street. The house is still there, just barely escaping the destruction occasioned by the building of a giant earthen dyke to spare the town repeated flooding. Highway traffic roars atop the berm, named The Bob Madon Bypass in honor of the town's Mayor-For-Life, who worked tirelessly to put the place back together after the utterly devastating flood of 1977.

Underneath the earth and rocks of the dyke, under the concrete of the modern highway, are remnants of The Warrior's Path, Boone's Trace, Wilderness Road, Kentucky Road, Dixie Highway…all now totally obliterated. The haze that billows along is not dust raised by Indian moccasins or by hooves of stagecoach horses, but diesel smoke from 16-wheeler trucks. US25E has become a four-lane superhighway.

The route was first trod by Ice Age animals including mastodons and the giant sloth (whose Latin name includes a reference to Thomas Jefferson, fascinated by the mysterious remains of giant animals found at Big Bone Lick in northern Kentucky, just south of where the glaciers stopped). Later trails were made by modern-era woodland bison, elk, and deer, and by the Shawnee and Cherokee who hunted them; then by Long Hunters, lost in the deep forest who-knows-where, gone a year or more, competing with Indians for game, returning with horse-loads of bison and beaver pelts and deer and elk hides, tanned in creek bottoms with animal brains, and with chestnut, oak, and hickory bark…carcasses left to rot in places which still bear names like Greasy Creek and Stinking Creek. This is the countryside where, around every bend, at least up to a few decades ago, every barn was decorated with signs, CHEW MAIL POUCH…BRUTON'S DENTAL SNUFF…SEE ROCK CITY. Many warned then, and some still do, of Armageddon: ARE YOU SAVED? GET RIGHT WITH GOD! JESUS IS COMING SOON!

The route curves around the valley to The Water Gap, a dramatic thousand-foot-deep gorge…a *cleft* sliced through the middle of Pine Mountain. We called it The Narrows, and this remains its local name today. Indians and Long Hunters called the Gap '*Wasioto*' [written in French as *Ouasioto*, and shown on 18th-century maps of the area], meaning [scholars think!] in Shawnee, or maybe in Wyandot, no one is quite sure, '*land where deer are plentiful*.' The name designated both the Gap and the rich hunting lands of The Cumberland Plateau, to which it gave access.

Between 1780 and 1810, some 300,000 pioneer settlers passed through. A Tollgate to raise money for the upkeep of 'The Kentucky Road,' was located where Clear Creek flows into the river just at the beginning of The Gap. Slowly, a village grew up beside the Gate, houses clinging precariously to the riverbank, cabins, stores, and stables, strung out a mile or more from The Narrows to where the river runs wide and water becomes so shallow people and horses can wade across. The ford-ing-place gave the village its earliest name, 'Cumberland Ford.' This was a place where settlers camped as they waited for the river to drop. The Tollgate was moved to the Ford after 1830.

Dr. Thomas Walker of Albemarle County, Virginia…founder of Charlottesville, physician, surveyor, frontier aristocrat and supremely successful speculator…mapped the area in 1750, when he explored an 800,000-acre grant of land to The Loyal Company, a group of tobacco-slave barons with influential connections in Williamsburg. The final entry in Walker's *Journal* reads: '*We killed in the journey 13 buffaloes, 8 Elks, 53 Bears, 20 Deers, 4 Wild Geese, about 150 Turkeys, besides small game. We might have killed three times as much meat, if we had wanted it.*'

Walker and his fellow-speculators gained control of thousands of acres. The wealth and prestige of English Lords and Dukes and Earls was based on huge estates. But New World Colonials could also play that game, and did. They were adept in acquiring vast estates…by '*treaty*' with Indians, midnight appropriation, or, easiest of all if they were politically influential, by simply 'granting' each other gigantic tracts in the unknown Wilderness which lay just over the western mountains. [See *Gateway: Dr. Thomas Walker and the Opening of Kentucky*, David M. Burns, Bell County Historical Society, Box 1344, Middlesboro, KY 40965, Telephone (606) 242-0005].

Walker writes in his **Journal**, '*Indians have lived about this Ford some years ago*,' alluding to the burial mound four hundred yards from the Ford. The top of the mound was removed in 1900 to make a flat space for H.C. Broughton's mansion, raising it high enough to escape flooding. (In 1938, when he and I were about ten and we were Cub Scouts beginning to become interested in such things, Ray Broughton and I dug into the clay of the house's unfinished basement and discovered Indian arrowheads, which we showed with pride to our Pack. I wonder where those arrowheads are today?) The mansion was torn down and the rest of the mound was removed in 1987 to make room for a Kentucky Fried Chicken restaurant. *No stopping Progress!*

The 1928 hospital is located three hundred yards from the place where the river breaks free from The Water Gap, receives substantial input from Straight Creek, and curves around the floodplain, which, When I Was A Boy, we always called The Gibson Farm. This is the fertile bottom land, enriched by topsoil deposited by floods, acquired by Virginia Military Warrant more than two centuries ago by Colonel Isaac Shelby, Kentucky's first Governor; who sold it to James Renfro; who sold it to J.J. Gibson, whose family name was foisted on, or adopted by, the handful of colored [the word we used in the 1930s, and which, so far as I was aware, did not give offense] families in Pineville, descendants of the slaves Gibson bought and hauled in to work his farm; a 'slave cabin' was still there a few years ago.

The river makes another loop at Wallsend, but from The Ford onward, gathers water in a more leisurely fashion than on the south side of Pine Mountain. Now, mostly liberated from the valley it has carved, both confinement and outlet, it continues to meander. But its course is now more purposeful, more confident, northward and westward toward Flat Lick, Barbourville, and the unique moon-bow of Cumberland Falls.

My mother told me that December 1, 1928 was a Saturday and that I was born at 4:00 p.m. She was twenty years old. She talked at length as early as I can remember, and repeatedly until her death at age 87, September 20, 1995, about how much she suffered during my birth.

The physician was Charles B. Stacy, twenty-seven, just starting out after a couple of years as doctor in the mining camp at Kettle Island, a few miles up Straight Creek. He was Pineville's leading surgeon for the next fifty years, and by the time of his death in 1983, was wealthy...at least by local standards, having steadily expanded the Hospital, of which he was chief owner. He used his money for hunting trips to Alaska and Africa, bringing back grisly trophies, perhaps symbolic of a surgeon's penchant for bloody intervention. Pineville Community Hospital is today a fairly imposing complex, just inside the floodwall opposite Wallsend. It gets its income from Medicare, Medicaid, Social Security Disability, Black Lung payments, and United Mine Worker health benefits for retired miners and their kinfolk.

'Suffer' was one of Louise's favorite words. She didn't seek pain; she wanted, simply, to be a good person; a good wife, a good mother; but she did suffer. I do not, and never would, imply that she was not in pain then, or later with a half-dozen chronic ailments; only that to her, pain, or any kind of misfortune, was personal, something she did not deserve, as though God or Fate had singled her out, had selected her like the notorious SS physicians at Auschwitz, as a plaything on which to inflict especially awful cruelties, both physical and mental.

She viewed herself, correctly I think, as a good person and very well intentioned. She was extremely proud of her ethical standards. 'I had every opportunity when I was bookkeeper for The Modern Bakery and for Smith-Cawood Hardware, to slip away with cash. I never did, and I never would. I'd work as long as it took to make those books balance right down to the very last PENNY!'

She felt aggrieved by the pain she suffered during childbirth. She was disappointed, she was angry. She, who 'never said a harsh word against anyone'; she, who, given her father's wealth, tragically 'stolen' decades earlier from her widowed Mother, had every right to expect better from life, had been tricked and deceived. It wasn't fair. She never lost that sense of injustice and saw herself throughout her life as Doomed to Suffer. She was a victim; suffering was her lot; it was simply Not Fair.

Even when I was still in short pants, she went into clinical detail, trying to make me understand, though I was so naïve about anatomy I did not really understand until I was seventeen and in an Air Force uniform, that she had been 'cut' by the physician. She had suffered when she was carrying me, suffered for a day and a half in the 'agony' of labor; she suffered then, and even when she was an old woman, and I not so young myself, she still angry that the doctor had 'cut' her.

It was doubtless unconscious and something she did not intend, but the effect was to make me feel guilty of a horrible crime, an unspeakable offense I had committed even before I was born.

I was confused. I did not WANT to make her suffer. What had I done? To confound me further, there was absolutely no way I could ever atone for this crime, and my guilt could never, ever, be expunged. This was Original Sin, big time. As a fetus and baby, innocently, unaware, and with no ability to avert it, I had caused my Mother immense suffering.

Seventy-three years later!, white hair fringing a large expanse of bald pink scalp...I acknowledge her suffering. But do I understand it? Do I understand its effect on me? Does the guilt she led me to assume, even though she did not intend it, underlie the free-floating guilt I still harbor?

Of course, my father also caused Louise heartache and agony. But so did I. Perhaps my feeling of guilt was and is justified.

JUDGE MITCHELL BURNS
MARCH 25, 1900–
DECEMBER 26, 1946

◆

My father was born in Pineville, the son of John Burns (1865-1924) and Mahala ('Haley') Garrett (1873-1924). H.H. Fuson's *History of Bell County* (Vol. 1) says 'the first man who settled on the level ground at the mouth of Mill Creek (above Kettle Island) was James Burns. He had two sons: William Burns and James Burns Jr. Bill Burns had a son, Davis Burns. He built two sawmills and gristmills on Straight Creek, near Burns' Spring and at Murphy Ward's place. He went to the Big Sandy River and built mills there. He sawed the lumber on Straight Creek that went into the old Court House in old Pineville in the Narrows. This was Bell County's first court house.' Bell County death records of 1878 note the death at age 75 from 'fever' of William Burns. The record says that he was born in Bell County, and that his parents were James and Elizabeth Burns.

William may have been the grandfather of John Burns (1865-1924). T.R. Ware's history of Cumberland Ford in *The Bell County Story* (1967) says that 'John Burns [possibly the father of John Burns, born 1865] was a member of the first Josh Bell County Fiscal Court, which met in 1867 in the home of C.C. Brittain, with Lewis F. Payne, county judge; James

H. Lee, county clerk; and C.B. Brittain, deputy clerk.' Mr. Ware cites M.G. Jones' survey and plat of 1867. This shows old Pineville extending 'from a point near where the old residence of John Burns now stands…' on or near Cumberland Avenue, toward the Narrows. Bell County marriage books A and C note that 'John Burns, justice of the peace,' performed marriage ceremonies in 1868 and 1870. These may be references to John 'Johnny' Burns (18??-18??) who married Rose Anne 'Annie' Lefevers (18??-19??). They had five children: Nan, William, Betsy, Bob, and John. In old age, Annie Lefevers Burns made her home with her son, my grandfather John. She lived to be 90, and her granddaughter, Josie, remembers her sitting on the porch, tatting beautiful lace, which she sold. Nancy Knuckles Garrett, the mother of John Burns' wife Mahala, also made her home with her daughter and son-in-law, in her old age.

My grandfather John Burns could not read or write, though friends told his daughter, Josie, that he was 'the smartest man in town. If he had had an education, he might have owned half of Bell County.' Mahala handled the paperwork connected with his business, which was buying and selling horses and mules (at one time he owned 44), and real estate, including rental property. He kept all his records in his head. No one could ever fool him about numbers. He had no need to write the figures down; he calculated in his head. He handled most of Pineville's drayage work, employing gangs of men to drive his wagons: an illiterate 'hillbilly' had managed to become a prosperous horse-and-wagon wrangler and 'A Man of Property', despite a total lack of book 'larnin'.

But after his death, two of his sons, budding alcoholics, the third a definite ne'er-do-well, soon dissipated his estate. Inman, the youngest, was a con man that managed to bilk many people, including his three wives, out of anything he could get. He also forged checks and stole money, for which he served time in the Ohio penitentiary. Louise and Judge were always apprehensive when Inman came around, which, since we had nothing of value, was, thankfully, seldom.

My grandfather John was five feet six inches in height, his wife almost five feet eleven. He had a small 'corporation' belly and an imposing, if ragged, mustache. He usually wore a black suit and white shirt, no tie. He always kept candy in his pockets, which he gave to children, who nicknamed him 'Candy John.' John and Mahala are buried in Pineville's Odd Fellows cemetery.

I don't know why my father was named 'Judge' or 'Mitchell.' Louise told me the Judge part was the name of a physician his mother had heard of. He began work with the Adams (later, Railway) Express Agency in 1917. He was just seventeen and not yet graduated from High School; so many men had volunteered for the Army there was a labor shortage. He was hired because of his excellent penmanship, which was expected, even demanded, then...but is little valued today. He was hired especially for his math skills, a talent he shared with his father, his brother Jim and his sister Rose. Excellent arithmetic was essential before calculators. [Information about John Burns' children, James, Rose, Josie, Judge, Rob and Inman, can be found in *Bell County Kentucky History and Families*, Bell County Historical Society, Middlesborough, 1994.]

Jim's son explained this family talent: 'Dad could add, in his head, a full page of five digit figures and simply write the total, from left to right, at the bottom of the column. He did it without hesitation or much apparent effort. He could add three digit columns, several pages in length, the same way.' I never observed my father quite as closely, probably because by the age at which I might have paid attention to such matters, he was no longer a Clerk and no longer in Pineville. But from what I do remember, and thanks to tiny fragments from Louise's 'archive,' I know that Judge was as gifted in math as his siblings.

I especially remember his bold handwriting. He usually wrote with a pencil, as he had to press through to make carbons of shipping and billing notices; he sharpened the pencil with a pocketknife. He also used ink, but always with a steel quill and an open pot, never a fountain pen, which the Express Agency did not provide and he could not afford. At work, Judge usually wore a white shirt and a four-in-hand necktie, though I don't think this was required. His fellow-employees also did not wear uniforms. But the truck drivers, like Alec Kellems, wore a cap with a lacquered bill, the crest of the cap embellished with the red diamond logo, 'Railway Express.' A few years ago in Washington's Union Station, at a store selling memorabilia of The Age of Steam, I spotted an enameled-tin red diamond logo…'Railway Express.' Of course, I HAD to have it: it's now on the wall of our kitchen.

The Railway Express Office was located underneath the two Waiting Rooms, one for 'White,' one for 'Colored,' of the Passenger Terminal of the Louisville & Nashville Railroad. The tracks snaked along the north bank of the Cumberland: to get to the Terminal one had to cross the river via a rickety steel bridge, a continuation of the town's main street, Kentucky Avenue. The L&N reached Pineville and Wasioto in 1888. For reasons that are today difficult to understand, the line then turned south to Middlesborough [often spelled today as 'Middlesboro'], and from there to Norton in Virginia…ignoring the rich timber and coal deposits of the upper Cumberland Valley in Harlan County.

Railroad spurs snaked outward as new coal camps sprang up, sometimes several in a single month, across the Cumberland Plateau. Soon steel rails linked every creek and holler in Bell County, and twenty years later in Harlan County…at least those hollers that had coalmines.

Even as a toddler with my Mom by my side, I went often to visit my father at the Railway Express office. The L&N Terminal was by far the most interesting place in town. For several decades, say 1915-1955…for our little town, and for most other towns across America…the railroad station was the source of never-ending and free entertainment. For a child, and I think also for adults, it was a wonderful pageant. I enjoyed every single bit of it, even mundane things like the telegrapher, with his hand key and Morse code, and the Ticket Office.

I particularly admired the engine drivers, dressed in their special black-and-white striped overalls, red bandana at the neck, on their head a soft cap adorned with their impressive job title and the L&N logo. The fireman's job, of course, was to shovel coal into the fire-bed from the tender in back of the engine and 'keep up a head of steam' in the boiler. The engineer and fireman, perched high up in the windows of the engine cab, would lean out first one side then the other, peering in the distance up the track, then back toward the cars of their train. They appeared to be lolling, seemingly nonchalant, though THEY were the ones in charge; THEY were the ones who made this giant machine *GO*!

A very rare, very special, treat, was riding in the locomotive cab from the Passenger Depot up North two miles, to the switching tracks at Wallsend. In my child's-mind I remember it as a frequent occurrence, but in fact I think it happened only a few times, as it was strenuously discouraged by the L&N, though the engineers and firemen got a big kick out of it.

Conductors and Signalmen, even the Ticket-Seller and the Telegrapher, were attired in natty blue serge suits, the L&N logo embroidered on the lapels, vests adorned with gold watch chains and fobs, totems of membership in The Masons, The Elks, The Odd Fellows. They consulted their large, ponderous pocket watches, special Railroad Models made by Hamilton and Waltham, with an air of grave importance. They were well aware of the drama, which they relished. 'Working on the railroad' was A GOOD JOB!

The long coal trains awed me then, and still do. Some comprised well over a hundred gondolas and stretched more than a mile in length. There were also maintenance trains with steam shovels, cranes, and gangs of rough workmen, manhandling heavy rails and sledgehammering thick spikes. I balanced myself, walking along the rail tops, or skipping along the oak crossties, kicking the gravel track bed. I was once taken for a joy ride, and WHAT JOY!, on a handcart, 'rowed' along by two men pushing down, pulling up, on a huge lever.

Of course, the real SPECTACLE, almost a sound-and-light show, was provided by the giant locomotive engines, ponderous and imposing black iron cylinders studded with mysterious and almost-certainly-dangerous pipes and valves [who KNEW what they did!?], pistons bleeding white steam, the smokestack throwing a long plume of black smoke and sparks, the fire-bed glowing red in the night or in the dark before dawn…The railroad was a thrilling fantasy-world.

People in Pineville, young or old, could instantly decipher the low, sustained whistles, the sounds flowing for MILES up and down our valley. 'That's the morning six-forty-five; it left last night from Louisville. That's the seven-oh-ten, up from Norton.' The whistles were a public time system. Whistles announced the arrival and departure of the two morning passenger trains, and warned us kids that we would soon be roused from bed. The whistles even told us how much time we had left to get dressed for school. Toward the close of the day, we knew it was getting on toward suppertime when we heard the whistles the two late-afternoon passenger trains, one going north to Louisville or Cincinnati, the other east toward Harlan or Norton.

Even after the passenger trains were through for the day, and as I lay in bed, I heard the whistles of coal trains, chugging through the night, the sound evoking a child's half wake/half dream image of smoke and steam. If it was VERY late, and if the house was quiet enough, I also heard, very faintly, a rhythmic Clack! Clack!…the sound carrying perhaps a full mile across the valley from where I lay…as steel wheels rattled over the rail-joints.

I often walked to The Terminal with my Mom even before I was old enough to go to school. When I was older, after school was over, I went almost every day by myself. As long as I did nothing dangerous, my Dad was happy to let me hang out with him. I watched everything and I loved it all, the arrival and departure of the trains, the noisy, complicated coupling and uncoupling of passenger and freight cars, engines and cabooses, the bustle of the Express Office.

I remember many happy times, times when Judge was sober, times when the day was warm and sunny. I remember us heading back home together, me on roller skates, going backward (so proud of myself, skating BACKWARD!) down the sidewalk of Kentucky Avenue. When we lived in Wallsend, Judge and I rode home a few times in the caboose of a coal train. The trains always stopped there two miles north of the Passenger Terminal, to take on water before heading off toward Crab Orchard and The Bluegrass. This stop was where Judge and I got off and walked the quarter-mile to our house.

Churches were, and still are, the center of all social life in our town. There was the big, thriving Baptist church, whose pastor, L.C. Kelly, inspired by the mountaineer's fervor of faith but appalled at the ignorance and illiteracy which made it impossible for those who had been 'called' to read The Bible, had started The Mountain Preacher's Bible School at Clear Creek. Others were The Methodist Church, The Disciples of Christ [Christian Church], Presbyterians, the Nazarenes, and a tiny Catholic church. The 'colored' worshipped at an A.M.E. [African Methodist Episcopal] church on Tennessee Avenue. You never saw any 'colored' in the 'white' churches on Sunday mornings. Church socials, Church picnics, festivals of 'Faith in Song,' baptisms…especially the public ones in the river, the many 'revivals'…these events punctuated the year. The churches served as our grapevine, a never-ending source of gossip, some of it accurate.

Pineville had, when I was a boy, a surprisingly literate weekly, *The Sun & Cumberland Courier* ['Bell County's Oldest Newspaper']. The Editor, Herndon Evans, was so sharp he later rose to be Editor of *The Lexington Herald-Leader,* and his name adorns The Lodge at Pine Mountain State Resort Park. I thought the linotype machine at *The Sun* was the most complicated mechanism I had ever seen, and I was totally fascinated. I edged up as close as the operator would allow, his fingers dancing across an arcane keyboard. After a line of molds for type had fallen into place, he would tip the bubbling pot of lead into the molds.

This produced a line of type. He then bundled the lines and locked them into forms, ready to be inked and printed. I was once given 'a line' as a souvenir. Of course the words were BACKWARDS, but the linotype operators could decipher them instantly.

The first and most SERIOUS! instruction I received on my first day as a copyboy at *The Evening Star* in Washington, was, 'Don't even THINK! of touching a piece of type; don't LOOK at it! The type belongs to the 'factory' guys that run the machines. *You are Editorial.* If you so much as TOUCH a piece of type, the Union guys will Walk Off The Job, and we'll have no paper at all!'

I also tagged along when Judge went to pay money, or, more often, borrow money, from Joe Liford, who had an office above The Coffee Pot Lunch and charged 'only ten per cent' [ten per cent *a week*!]. We also went to the imposing mansion occupied by Pineville's other lender-of-last-resort, Bill Hays, whose terms were identical to Liford's...except that Hays required Louise, or, better yet, Judge's well-heeled brother Jim, who had risen from Clerk to Superintendent of the imposing Wisconsin Steel coal operation at Benham, to co-sign a Note.

During the worst years of The Depression, one of my jobs was to operate a little machine to roll cigarettes for Judge, using of course the cheapest tobacco available, not really leaf at all, just stalks and auction-floor sweepings sold in tiny cotton bags. Judge was also addicted [perhaps a more precise term would be 'dependent on'] caffeine. He would drink as many as twelve cups of coffee a day, and given his jumpy nervous tension, I cannot see how this could have been a good idea. I thought of him when I saw ads in the comic strips of the 1930's for Sanka, just then coming on the market; the central feature of the ad was 'Mr. Coffee Nerves.'

Judge also had one affliction which I have never heard of since: when he was drunk, which was at least once every two weeks, he would often begin to yawn uncontrollably...huge yawns, his mouth so agape his jaws would *snap!, locked wide-open.* This caused immediate and severe pain, but there was simply no way he could get his jaws closed again. Fifty years later, I asked 'young' Doctor Wilson (who was by this time well past eighty!) about this. He said, 'I treated Judge several times. His jaws were so painful I had to give him a little chloroform to get them closed.' [*The Merck Manual* suggests this is an 'internal tempomandibular derangement'; 'lockjaw without infection' sounds simpler.]

Judge suffered for years with nausea, stomach pain, and other intestinal problems, dosing himself with bicarbonate of soda, AlkaSeltzer, SalHepatica, Bisodol, Scalf's Indian River Tonic, and many other patent medicines. The only effect, so far as I could tell, was a series of noisy burps. (Today, fifty-six years after his death, I feel fairly confident that his nausea and abdominal pain were symptoms of chronic pancreatitis, a common result of alcoholism, and was almost certainly the precursor of his fatal cancer of the pancreas.)

Judge was as addicted to debt as he was to alcohol. The two fed off each other. He often didn't have a cent when re-payment was due, and his creditors regularly attached or garnisheed his wage. This, of course, meant a 'payless pay-day,' no money for rent or food, and required him to borrow from somebody else, if he could FIND somebody else. Most often, he moved out his family just as rent was due and before our furniture was 'set out in the street.'

We were poor, *though Judge had a job!*, and we were certainly nowhere near as poor as most in Appalachia in The Depression. Some of the MANY houses we lived in were pretty rough, but we were never without some kind of home, and I don't remember ever going to bed hungry.

I once tried to make an inventory of the places we lived in from 1928 to 1943: the first I remember was the little house on Cumberland Avenue (I think it had been owned, and perhaps had been left to him, by Judge's father). Then, the house owned by 'old Dr. Wilson,' where the A&P was later located. I remember that house particularly; I was about two, and we had just moved in; there were mothballs in some of the woolen things, and I thought they gave off the most interesting smell I had yet encountered. I started sniffing, kept on SNIFFING! and soon had the ball lodged up high inside my nostril. This required a trip to the doctor. I can't quite remember how, but he got it out.

This was also the house we were living in when I heard excited talk about the river 'in flood.' I had no idea what that *meant*, but it seemed interesting and I thought I ought to go down and check it out. Louise was sick with worry and sent out a General Alarm. I walked three blocks down Pine Street to the bridge, and was heading toward the water, when somebody saw me and hauled me back. I didn't get far from Louise's sight after that!

A year or so later, we lived in an apartment in what had been The Pineville Hotel, built about 1900 when there was hope that the little town might become prosperous, the center of a coal boom; but the old Hotel had fallen into disrepair. There was only one bathroom per floor, so we had to use a slop jar at night, which was humiliating then, and a little humiliating even in the recollection of it.

We lived in a stucco house next to the Presbyterian Church and across the street from T.J. Asher's white-columned mansion; his grand-kids tried to drown me, or at least I thought they were trying to drown me!, in the goldfish pond in their backyard. The stucco house was torn down many years ago and the lot is now used for the annual Breakfast offered by the Pineville Community Hospital to kick off the Saturday parade and pageant of the Kentucky Mountain Laurel Festival.

We lived in a little apartment in the I.L. Hopkins Building on Virginia Avenue; and later, across the street, in an apartment above Dr. Edward Wilson's office, that is, 'young Doc Wilson.' This one had only a kerosene stove; I cannot imagine how Louise could possibly have cooked on such a contraption. A flood brought water halfway up to the second floor where we lived; there were rowboats in the streets. Later, we lived in a frame house across from the feed store and the garage housing the bulldozers and other equipment of the Kentucky Highway Department.

We also lived in a frame house in Wallsend, perhaps no more than a hundred yards from the river. Louise cooked on a cast-iron stove, and managed to turn out good meals; my job was to haul in the coal, and keep the fire going. Her refrigerator was, like most in the early 1930s, an icebox: the ice company supplied a square, the corners of which said 25, 50, 75, or 100, indicating the size of the block you wanted. We kids would follow the ice wagon, enjoying the slivers as the big block was chipped into the correct size. I liked that house maybe most of all.

Like everyone in The Depression, Louise haunted the Church rummage sales, scrounging for anything useful, such as clothing that might fit Dick or me. If someone had more apples or blackberries or black walnuts than they could use, or if someone had gathered more dandelions or wild greens than they could cook up, and offered some, Louise would gladly accept, though she was far too proud to ASK.

I remember the walnuts fondly. We were living in The Pineville Hotel, and there were many bushels of FREE nuts. Only trouble was, you had to get the green husks off, which meant your hands and clothing were stained brown for weeks. But I didn't mind. It was a warm summer night, just getting dark, and fireflies were EVERYWHERE! blinking a code only they understood. I did not understand the code, but I sure enjoyed firefly lights, and still do.

Louise was not selective in her frugality: she simply saved EVERYTHING!, a pack-rat trait that made her sister Rachel furious. Rachel would drive down from Black Mountain in their *current-year* Buick sedan, which seemed to me the ritziest car in the world, a totem of their wealth. And Rachel would simply TEAR into Louise's house, throwing out this, chucking that, burning stuff in the back yard, ranting a mile-a-minute about Louise's pack rat ways, which Louise was, of course, unable to stop. I believe Rachel sincerely believed she was HELPING Louise by disposing of mountains of JUNK.

But Louise was offended, humiliated.

I confess I did the same thing sixty years later. My only excuse: a small apartment can only HOLD so much! Louise never lost that Depression-era survival skill. When I helped her move from her first Washington apartment, and from her second apartment to an assisted-living home, I discovered STUFF...*mountains* of STUFF!...all neatly stacked, box after box, every one tied with ribbons. I feel sure Louise had no clear idea WHY she laboriously saved empty boxes and empty jars.

And was she ever a FANATIC about clean! She would wash the dishes, but if they had been 'out' for a couple of hours, would wash them all over again. The Germ Theory of Disease was BIG NEWS as Louise was growing up; was that the cause of her obsessive compulsion to clean? Or perhaps she had, as the psychiatrists delicately put it, a tendency toward the 'anal-retentive'?

She scrimped on herself so she could provide for her kids. I was pretty much spoiled rotten. I think I was treated like Duke Ellington, who said 'my Mother never allowed my feet to touch the floor.' Louise dressed me in neat corduroy knickers and Buster Brown shoes. Once I got a BRAND-NEW (not second-hand, not from a rummage sale, but NEW!) navy blue, wool jacket. I am deeply ashamed, SEVENTY YEARS LATER!, that on my way to second grade, while watching, completely fascinated, as WPA workmen applied roofing to the new Post Office, I brushed up against the hot tar-pot and got black tar on my BRAND-NEW coat! I cried so hard I thought my lungs and eyes would crack. Louise was heart-broken; there is simply no way, in the worst depths of The Depression, a Mother can afford to buy a SECOND, new, good-looking, warm wool jacket!

She cooked fudge and divinity candy; she made wonderful corn-bread, and pinto bean soup. I still have no idea how this poverty-stricken family managed it, but I found under our Christmas trees things like a Tom Mix pistol, an electric train, a chemistry set, Lincoln logs. I spent hours with straight pins and Testor's glue, trying to fabricate model airplanes out of balsa wood kits (some actually flew, but never more than a few feet). I made a soap-box-derby car out of skate wheels. I tinkered with crystal radios and constructed breadboard radios (which ALMOST worked; at least I heard static). I made and flew kites. I made a pinhole camera, but never got a single image from it. I had a puppy, 'Pep,' who licked my face and liked to sleep next to me, which I loved. But he got loose from our I.L. Hopkins apartment and was run over in the street.

Louise also wangled me a part in the Mountain Laurel Festival, started by Annie Walker Burns, married to Judge's cousin Hargis. Annie Walker Burns had proposed that Dr. Thomas Walker [whose *Journal* was the first written record of Kentucky exploration] be honored by an annual event at Pineville. She was an indefatigable genealogist, and hoped she might be descended from Dr. Walker, but was never able to make a clear connection. She did, however, compile several books, including an exhaustive record of Walker's descendants, published as *Doctor Thomas Walker, First White Man of Any Distinction to Explore Kentucky*.

Because of her determination (and her access to Governor Flem Sampson, for whom she worked as clerk-typist), she was able to get things going. Shouldn't the State Honor its first explorer? Shouldn't these beautiful mountains be the venue for the Celebration? The first two Festivals, in 1931 and 1932, were held at Clear Creek Baptist Bible College, an appropriate site, since Walker had camped on 'Clover Creek' [today, Clear Creek], which he followed to its confluence with a river, which he named 'The Cumberland.' In 1933 the event was moved to Laurel Cove, a natural amphitheater in Pine Mountain State Resort Park. The Park had just opened, thanks to T.J. Asher's gift of land, and hard work by CCC crews of strong, but of course unemployed, young men. At age two and again at three, I was a 'pillow bearer,' dressed in white satin shorts, in the pageant that crowned The Queen of The Kentucky Mountain Laurel Festival.

I was about the same age when my Mom began to take me with her to Gragg's Rexall Drugstore, where someone would lift me onto the marble soda fountain or a tabletop, where I would sing in a little-boy soprano. The customers rewarded me with coins, at first a penny or two per song, later upped to a nickel each…quite a thrill then, and maybe a little thrill even now, remembering it.

The tunes I recall are 'My Buddy,' always requested by grizzled veterans of Chateau-Thierry, 'There's A Gold Mine In The Sky,' 'The Umbrella Song,' 'M.O.T.H.E.R' and 'My Mom.' These last two invariably caused every mother within hearing to tear up. I also sang solos in The First Christian Church, egged on by our long-time choirmaster (and the town's Assistant Postmaster), Paul Greene. He was a tenor, and sang quite well; I was flattered that he thought I could sing, too.

The singing TOOK, and I'm still at it. But I'm afraid that as far as church is concerned, I'm a total failure, not only a 'back-slider' and sinner, but what is far, far worse, a Secular Humanist! [Which reminds me of a line Claude Pepper used to great effect when he was, yet again, running for re-election to the Senate: 'Folks, I know you'll find this hard to believe, but *my opponent is a flagrant THESPIAN!*' Pepper won, of course. Florida voters were not about to have any *thespian* represent them!]

My schoolteachers, especially Paul's sisters Mollye and Laura Greene, were impressed with my incessant, compulsive reading. Other teachers I remember fondly are Effie Arnett, an effective teacher of English, and Alva Tandy, a legendary teacher of algebra and geometry…strict, but deeply respected, even LOVED!, by every child she ever taught.

There was another teacher; I wish I could remember her name, who came to class fairly often wearing a thin silk blouse and NO BRA. Her 'mams' bounced appropriately, which was of course utterly FASCINAT-ING for every boy in the class. I will never know whether she did this on purpose, whether it was a hot day and she wanted to wear as little as possible, or if she just was late, and had no time to put on all her clothing. I strongly suspect she enjoyed 'teasing' pubescent boys.

The town had a swimming pool located between the football end zone, and the river; I loved to swim, but I was too chicken to attempt the daredevil jackknifes and twirls the athletic kids displayed. But of course I ogled the girls, trying to figure out basic anatomy. At that age, I still couldn't make it out. If I had grown up on a farm, there would have been no uncertainty! When we were living above the office of 'young Dr. Wilson' and I had been hired to sweep the floors and dust his office, I peeked into a copy of *Gray's Anatomy;* there was no one around to stop me. But it was too much for me to absorb; I remained naïve.

Our three-story school had one feature I don't recall seeing elsewhere: the fire escape looked like a silo; it held a slick metal slide, the purpose of which was, presumably, to get more kids out of the building faster and safer. We kids loved the slide just for the whirly sensation of it. Since we enjoyed it, the principal naturally locked the doors to the escape. I have no idea what would have happened if there been an actual FIRE!

I read constantly, even while eating, and thought I would invent some kind of clear plastic tray, so the text of a book could be projected right onto your 'plate'; that way you wouldn't have to avert your eyes from the page *for even a second.* I also read while walking down the street, and it's a miracle I never fell into an open manhole. I read anything and everything: all the type on the cereal boxes, train tickets, Big Little Books from the dime store, every magazine on the racks in the drugstores.

I once set a goal: I would read EVERY book in our town's little Library, housed next to the City Jail. With encouragement from our able Librarian, Clo Era Sewell, I very nearly made it. I read *The Swiss Family Robinson* at least five times straight through, plus Richard Halliburton' *Royal Road to Romance,* and every one of Halliburton's other glorious travel stories. I suspect this may have put a life-long groove in my brain, persuading me that the only worthwhile life was one of adventure and travel.

In the fifth grade, I decided for some reason, maybe just the challenge of it, that I would read *The World Book Encyclopedia* in our school's library. I started at the upper left-hand corner of Page One, and finished the entire thing before the end of the school year.

I was 'double-promoted' twice, a practice which was fairly common then, but which today inspires in me considerable doubt. The promotions gave me an exaggerated, and doubtless completely unwarranted, opinion of my intelligence. [It was simply ARROGANT, even for a child's limited understanding, to imagine that at age nine, or eleven, or thirteen, or fifteen, I could run away from home…which I did!…and somehow 'make it' on determination alone. Arrogance later got me into some serious trouble].

Skipping ahead put me in classes with kids a year or two older than I was, and bigger and stronger to boot. Timid and skinny, I didn't have the brawn or toughness to hold my own against bullying and teasing…common then and now, on grade-school playgrounds. The worst teasings I remember, and they happened fairly often (I don't know why the teachers never intervened), was being held down and tickled until I became completely hysterical. This was utterly **cruel**. The tickling by the bullyboys had me so nerve-shaken and out of control I should have been hospitalized. It took me hours to calm down.

It was impossible for my classmates to refrain from laughing when I stammered, which of course caused me to turn red and stammer even MORE. I don't blame them; I would have laughed myself; it must have been a real hoot! to see me struggling, my body tense with effort and my face contorted into a hideous knot, trying, trying to speak, to say something, ANYTHING! There were months at a time when I could not utter one single word without stuttering badly, and there were many times I could not be understood at all.

It's hardly surprising that I retreated to books. This, of course, led inexorably to aspirations…maybe I could become A WRITER! [Perhaps I am still 'retreating' today?]

Louise, ALWAYS A WORLD-CLASS WORRIER!, was terribly upset about my stuttering; she read everything she could find, but she never had any idea what, if anything, to do. She thought talking with marbles in my mouth might help; but that idea had died with Demosthenes. She suggested that I singsong my phrases, or speak more slowly, or e-nun-ci-ate. She sent me off to W.P. Slusher, a Pineville 'personality' who had made it big as 'Preston, Magician and Hypnotist.' 'Preston' gave it his best shot, in the hope that a post-hypnotic suggestion might cure my stammering. But he wasn't able to hypnotize me AT ALL, I suspect because of my sheer childish willfulness: 'I am stronger! He can't 'command' ME!'

Nothing Louise tried or others suggested ever worked, and I continued to stammer. Today, decades later, we still have little or no idea of the cause of stammering nor any effective way to correct it.

BUT I COULD *SING*!…and I never *EVER* stammered when I sang! One teacher said, 'David, why don't you just *SING* your recitation?'

I enjoyed music a lot, particularly under the tutelage of our school's music teacher, the beautiful and vivacious redhead, Miss Flossie Minter. I think she liked me; I sure liked her! She gave me a big part in the kiddies' musical 'Hansel and Gretel' by Englebert Humperdinck, a name later adopted by a British rock star. I was minutely investigating the machinery for opening and closing the curtains and for dimming the lights; Miss Arnett, exasperated, scolded me: 'David, you are A NUISANCE!' I replied, 'No, Miss Arnett, I am A WOOD SPRITE!'

But what should have been a source of pride, caused enormous humiliation. There were no dressing rooms in our school's auditorium, used mainly for Lyceum events. So, during the operetta, the boys were to put on their costumes on one side of the stage, the girls on the other. Okay. Understood. But when I went offstage, I somehow made a wrong turn and ended up where the girls were dressing! and I SAW SOME OF THEM IN THEIR UNDERWEAR! How awful! What a sneak! A Peeping Tom! I knew I had messed up BIG TIME, and burst out crying: 'I made a mistake! I made a mistake! I didn't do it on purpose! NOT ON PURPOSE!' I think I cried for a full half-hour. [An odd fact, possibly interesting but NOT germane, is that one of the girls was named 'George'; she later served with The Waves.]

I joined a Boy Scout troop led by Harrywood Gray, pastor of The Christian Church, and one summer spent a week, maybe two, at a Boy Scout Camp, perhaps…I can't remember clearly…Camp Blanton in Harlan County.

Using Reverend Gray's knowledge of carpentry, our Troop built a cabin in the woods above Clear Creek, on a hill above the L&N line to Chenoa. I wish it had been a LOG cabin; that would have been perfect. In fact, it was simply rough-sawn boards, which I suspect had been donated by a local sawmill. We went on hikes to the sandstone ridge atop Pine Mountain, which looked directly down on our town. From there, we climbed out onto Chained Rock for a dramatic view of the deep gorge of The Narrows.

In 1931, a bunch of 'the boys,' including some from The Rotary and Kiwanis Clubs, salvaged a giant chain from a dredge on the Tennessee River. It was hauled by mule-team up the mountain, where it was 'spiked' into a boulder that looked as though it might come tumbling down into The Narrows. The other end of the chain was anchored into the rock of the mountainside. That chain would no more have held that enormous rock than would a cotton thread! 'Chained Rock' was nothing more than a joke, something to *draw tourists*. Which is precisely what local folks had in mind.

We also climbed the mountain on our own. We were there alone when Jack Foley, a classmate and in my Troop, managed to get his body across the chain by holding on, first by one hand, then by the other. The chain was more than a hundred feet long, and he would have been dashed against the rocks far below had he fallen. Fifty years later, severely depressed, he committed suicide by leaping out the third-floor window of Pineville Hospital. Is it possible his life-long propensity for doing the most dangerous thing he could think of, was somehow connected to his tragic death?

From our high vantage point, cars appeared as small as ants; coal trains made long sinuous curves snaking 'round the bends of the river. We were up so high (or at least we thought we were) and everything looked so small and distant, the view seemed as unreal as a movie. We slept under Turtleback Rock, which I later learned had been used by ancient Woodlands Indians as a Rock Hotel.

This was wonderful Boy Scout territory: trails wandered through ravines choked with old-growth hemlock, oak, tulip poplar, fern gardens, waterfalls, and lichen-covered sandstone boulders. There were snakes, mostly harmless garter snakes and black snakes; there were salamanders, shrews, skunks, and 'possums. We saw no deer then, but they are today so common as to be a nuisance; turkey and bear have also returned. Spring and summer brought blossoms of Catawba and Great rhododendron, red azalea, mountain laurel [known to the first settlers as 'mountain ivy'], pink lady slipper, wild blueberries, huckleberries, serviceberry and flowering dogwood.

A perk of my Dad's job was a few free passes to ride the train. He and I made a couple of trips to Louisville to visit his sister Josie and brother Rob. I begged him to let us ride in the last car so I could stand on the open-air platform and watch the tracks as they receded into the distance. I also loved the sudden blackouts when we went through tunnels. I even enjoyed the soot and cinders from the engine that sometimes rained down.

Once, the two of us went to Cincinnati, arriving at the new Union Station there, the chief feature of which was a giant barrel arch like the Baths of Caracalla in Rome. We went up to take in a baseball game. Judge never played any kind of sport, but baseball was popular in the mountains and every mining-camp had a team. He followed baseball over the radio and was proud he could point out for me PeeWee Reese, star of The Cincinnati Reds.

My Dad's co-workers included Alec Kellems, Joe and Kenneth Shufflebarger and their sister, Dorothy, who I think worked only part-time, and the boss, Martin, always referred to as 'Old Man Shufflebarger.'

Judge had pale blue eyes and thick brown hair, with a nervous tic of running his hand through his hair, using his fingers as a coarse comb. He stood a bit under five-foot-nine, halfway in height between his somewhat pudgy father and his tall, gangly mother. He was stooped over, his back curved with a stoop so severe it would today be called sco-liosis, curvature of the spine. (Louise also had a severely curved spine even as a young woman, and to the end of her days kept hoping a physi-cian would 'fit' her with 'a garment' or brace to straighten her up; she was well aware that her posture put pressure on her innards.)

Judge was slightly built, his body comprised far more of nerves than of muscle. This was unfortunate, since, although technically a Clerk, he was expected to load and unload the Express cars on the trains. Many of the boxes were of enormous size, and some wooden crates weighed hundreds of pounds.

His first task was to manhandle these monsters off the Express car and onto the high, steel-wheeled platform wagons. Then he had to maneuver the wagons from the platform down a steep grade to the Express Office under the Passenger Terminal. Many times I felt sure the wagon was going to get away from him and perhaps crush us both. In the office, he would inspect the cartons and crates, noting day and hour of arrival and so on, verifying Manifests and Invoices. He would then help Alec or others get the crates up onto the truck and send the ship-ments off for delivery. He also drove the truck and made deliveries when other men were sick or off on vacation.

Judge's feet caused him frequent pain; he hobbled like a guy with bad feet: he had a mal-formed arch, plus multiple corns and bunions. He and Louise speculated that the concrete of the train platform and the concrete floor of the Express office caused his foot trouble. Whatever the cause, his feet always hurt and I never saw him walk with ease. He was a steady patron of Dr. Scholl's this-and-that.

Bad teeth were common throughout the South and extremely common in Appalachia, perhaps the result of poor diet, or, more likely, ignorance and poverty. A good set of teeth was such a rare sight as to be noticeable. Judge's bad teeth might have been exacerbated by his passion for candy or anything sweet, a craving perhaps inherited from his father, 'Candy John.' A few of Judge's teeth were missing entirely, rotted to the gum-line, those remaining pocked with black decay. His teeth caused him frequent pain, sometimes severe. I do not know why he never did anything about this. Perhaps, like most in Appalachia, he thought he could not afford to pay the dentist. I think it's more likely he was terrified of even worse pain in getting them repaired. (Louise also had terrible teeth, and by 1947 had none that could be saved; she summoned up her courage and had them all extracted, though her dentures bothered her for the remainder of her life.)

During the worst years of the Depression, the Express office had only part-time work, a few hours a day, a few days a week. Like many other breadwinners across the country, Judge simply HAD to find a way to bring in more income. He opened a newsstand in the storefront on Kentucky Avenue later occupied by Joe The Tailor, selling cigarettes, candy, chewing gum, magazines, and novelties. His biggest moneymaker was a game of chance, where you push a pin through thick cardboard, extract a tightly rolled paper with a number on it; if the paper has the right digits, you win a prize. Today, it would be Power Ball or Lotto.

He also borrowed H.D. Arterberry's car and tried hard, very hard, to sell vacuum cleaners door-to-door in areas of Bell County that, thanks to the Rural Electrification Administration, had just received electric service. I went with him on a couple of those trips, the car bouncing up and down creek beds, as there was no road whatsoever, dirt OR paved. We also walked across remote creeks, on bridges whose footpath was suspended from cables. So far as I can remember, Judge never sold a single machine; the problem was simple, fundamental: most people had no money *AT ALL*. I had the same no-sale no-luck experience in 1949 at Princeton when I tried to sell WebCor wire recorders, a device just then coming on the market, magnetic tape being several years in the future.

Judge also rented a vacant lot, about a quarter-acre, near a house we lived in across from the Feed and Grain store where Cumberland and Park Avenues join. The garden was one of his more successful Depression Era efforts. He hired a man to plow the field, but did everything else himself, planting, hoeing, weeding, harvesting, with me 'helping' as only a five-year-old can. Louise sweated through steamy summer nights, cutting up vegetables and canning them in Ball jars. To prevent spoilage, the process required precise temperatures and sterilization by boiling [Louise, with her cleanliness obsession, was A DEMON! on sterilization], and rubber-ring seals. That food kept us going another year. But Judge never planted anything again.

The most dramatic, even terrifying, incident that summer was when Judge, staggering, roaring…so drunk he was completely out of his mind, banged open the front door, and the minute he reached the kitchen, began to beat Louise as hard as he could. She was heavily pregnant with Dick, and unable to dodge his blows. I was not yet six; I don't know what I thought a child could do, but I was not about to let him beat her up…yet again! I grabbed a butcher knife off the counter and put myself between them. 'Stop it! Don't you hit my Mother!' Judge was startled, reeled drunkenly, stumbled, and fell into bed, passed out cold.

A similar incident occurred when we lived in Wallsend. At the time, I thought it might be the scene of a double murder…Judge, in a crazy drunken rage, beating Louise to death…me killing Judge in revenge.

Fortunately, this time I did not grab a butcher knife. Instead, I ran out of the house screaming. Neighbors called the police, and Pearl Osborne, Sheriff of our little town, showed up…sporting his trademark pearl-handled revolver. Judge was so drunk he could offer no resistance. The Sheriff escorted him to The Jail downtown to sleep it off. Judge was never charged with any crime, though it might have had a salutary effect on him if he had been.

Judge patronized the barbershop on Kentucky Avenue. I remember it mostly because of the shoe-shiner, a broken-backed 'colored' man (of course surnamed Gibson) with a wry sense of humor and a cracked treble laugh. After Judge was fired and left town, Louise could no longer afford to send me there. I was sent instead to a 'colored' barber who had a little shack at the end of Pine Street just before the bridge; he charged ten cents. Judge also introduced me to Blind George, who lived in a room above the pool hall at the corner of Kentucky Avenue and Pine Street, and who sold hotdogs on the street corner and at football and basketball games.

Judge liked music and could beat out good rhythm on the spoons. His favorite tune was 'Oh! How I Wish I Was in Peoria,' which he whistled through his teeth, not with puckered lips. He read the Cape Cod novels of Joseph Lincoln and a few by Zane Grey, and magazines like *Saturday Evening Post* and *Liberty*. I don't remember that we got a daily newspaper, but I do remember the Sunday comics of *The Cincinnati Enquirer*…Dick Tracy, Little Orphan Annie, Terry and The Pirates, Mutt and Jeff, The Katzenjammer Kids, Maggie and Jiggs ('Bringing Up Father').

We enjoyed listening to the radio, after we received The Philco, a 1935 Christmas gift from Louise's sister Rachel and her husband Bill. The set was shaped like the window of a Gothic cathedral, and functioned much like TV sets today, a surrogate family hearth. Our favorite station was WHAS out of Louisville, but we also listened to WLW in Cincinnati. I remember 'Edgar Bergen and Charlie McCarthy,' 'Amos and Andy,' 'Lum and Abner,' 'One Man's Family,' 'Mr. Keene, Tracer of Lost Persons' and others, like Bing Crosby, Eddie Cantor, and Kate Smith. I enjoyed a Saturday morning children's program, 'Coast To Coast On A Bus.'

I went to Saturday matinees at The Gaines Movie Theatre. Given my penchant for singing, I particularly enjoyed the glorious musicals of the 1930s, and remember many of them vividly, especially the sophistication of Fred Astaire and Ginger Rogers. I identified with the child singer Bobby Breen. And I wished I had Jane Withers' effervescence. I admired the singing of Bing Crosby and Dick Powell, and tried to capture in my mind their sound, what they did, so I could copy it. Maybe my mind is playing tricks on me, but I think I was able to sing both words and music from movies after a single hearing.

The most solemn moment in Judge's workweek, and also a Big Moment for me, was the bundling and dispatch of Railway Express documents and payments. The money was placed in a heavy kraft envelope, which Judge sealed, signing his name across both top and bottom flaps. The papers were of Shipments Received, Shipments Delivered, Hours Worked, Salaries Paid, and Payments and Cash Received. The package of documents was given to the senior Railway Express employee on the train, who signed a receipt book, and would deliver the package to the central Express office when the train arrived in Louisville. The envelope was solemnly sealed, its flaps fastened by red wax, the wax indented while still molten with 'THE SEAL' of the Pineville Railway Express Agency. Judge held the big kitchen match, but allowed me to melt the wax and push in The Seal. Wow! It still seems quite A Big Deal…even as I recollect across six decades.

But this memory also brings sadness and dismay. *The Envelope With The Big Red-Wax Seal* was the cause of Judge's downfall.

No, that's not right. The Envelope was THE MEANS of Judge's downfall. THE CAUSE was Terrible Judgment caused by drunken befuddlement. No, that's not quite right either.

Seven decades later, we may be a bit more enlightened, or, in my case, a bit more PERSONALLY SINGED, about drinking. Today we prefer a less pejorative term…It seems more 'correct' and is indeed more accurate, to say that Judge's downfall was caused by the disease of alcoholism.

When sober, which was perhaps ninety per cent of the time, he was an intelligent and kindly man, and a fine father. Booze changed him from a pleasant Dr. Jekyll, into a hideous beast, Mr. Hyde. Alcohol has the same effect on many today. I didn't hate him then, and I don't hate him now. But he would have been happier, and his wife and kids would have lived normal lives, even though dirt-poor in the middle of the Depression, had he been able to stop drinking.

Judge was with The Railway Express Agency from 1917 until 1941. He wanted to be a good husband and a good father. He searched for A Way, but genetic predisposition, or our Mountain Moonshine environment, or both, caused him to fail in his quest. In a small town EVERY-BODY knew within hours what had happened, and there was no possibility whatsoever of Judge finding work in Pineville. He fled to Louisville, hoping to find work, and promising to send for us when he had a job and place for us to live. But he never sent Louise any money after he left; she depended on Rachel and Bill for rent and food until she herself got a job…twenty cents an hour!

In Louisville, he lived with, and to a large extent off of, his sister Josie, who was at the time also boarding her alcoholic brother Rob, while trying to hold down a job and care for her husband, deathly ill with tuberculosis, complicated, as it so often is, by alcoholism.

My brother Dick and I went up to Louisville by train in 1942 to visit him. We slept on the floor, as the apartment was full up with three Arterberrys (Aunt Josie, her invalid husband H.D., and her precocious book-worm daughter Mary Jo, later a lawyer and Judge), plus Josie's brothers Rob and Judge. We all crowded into a little apartment in 'The Project,' a WPA housing development for people below the poverty line, which at that time was just about everybody, even though The War was beginning, slowly, to lift The Depression. I remember that Josie sent me to The White Tower to tote back a big bag of so-called 'hamburgers' ['buy 'em by the bag!']

Judge was at that time working as an attendant at a roller-skating rink. He took me there, and I saw him on his hands and knees, fitting skates and tightening them. He certainly didn't verbalize it, nor did I, but I sensed that he felt ashamed. He had lost a good, steady job, and in every way that mattered, had lost his family as well. He was now pretty much at the bottom of the heap, essentially unemployable. He was weak, hung-over, his hands trembling. This condition was normal for him in those days. I had no way of knowing…but he had only a few years left to live.

I wish I had asked more questions. But understanding does not cure alcoholism; Louise tried for years to 'understand.' By the time I saw him again, he was yellow with jaundice and only a few days away from death, with cancer of the pancreas (even today a diagnosis of doom). He was so dopey with morphine that conversation was impossible. He is buried in Resthaven Cemetery in Louisville. I wish we had talked more when we had the chance!

The simple sad truth is, Judge was utterly helpless around booze. He was an alcoholic of the intermittent, or 'binge,' variety. When he received his pay, I feel certain he left the Express office headed straight for home. He crossed the bridge, determined that 'this time' he would get there with his money intact.

But the folding bills in his pocket began to 'talk' to him. His feet hurt, his back hurt, his teeth hurt. He was angry that a man of his intelligence and education had to wrestle heavy crates for a living, and a poor living at that! When he got to the end of the bridge and saw the Blind Pig bootleg joints, his brain 'talked' to him loudly, and much more insistently. 'Just one. I can have Just One. Don't I *deserve* Just One? I work hard. *Just one.*'

A day later, sometimes three days later, he would stagger home, eyes bloodshot, clothing filthy. He was weak and trembling, sick as a dog…not one red cent left.

Louise often tried to head off disaster: I remember many occasions, so terribly humiliating for me, when she would send me up and down Pine Street, into all the dives. She herself, a respectable woman, would not dare enter, but since I was just a kid, she thought it was maybe okay. She told me what to say:

'Please, is my Daddy here? Has my Daddy *been* here? If you *see* my Daddy, *PLEASE*, please tell him to Come Home!'

Louise read in the newspaper about some 'special medicine' [I'm pretty sure it was Antabuse, just then beginning to be used]. The ad said you could put this stuff in someone's coffee, and if they subsequently took a drink of alcohol it would make them so sick they acquired an immediate aversion to booze and would never drink again. Louise thought long and hard about this. She even asked me: 'but suppose it makes him too sick to work? Suppose it *kills* him? I couldn't live with myself.'

In 1935, in Akron, Ohio, Bill W. and Dr. Bob had hit bottom and were desperate to save themselves. They stumbled onto a mutual-help system that is today ubiquitous. AA and its many offshoots have allowed millions to recover and live normal lives…not just the addicts themselves, but also those who love them and depend on them. It is sad that AA never reached our little town.

It might have saved Judge Burns.

LOUISE COOKE BURNS
JANUARY 14, 1908–
SEPTEMBER 20, 1995

———————◆———————

My mother was born in Middlesborough, just on the Kentucky side of Cumberland Gap. It was a quintessential boomtown, created in 1890 at the apex of The Gilded Age. It grew from the vision, or hype, of one man, Alexander Arthur. He was more developer than Robber Baron, but without doubt a super salesman. The fact that he was the nephew of President Chester Arthur gave him entrée. He made the most of it, persuading supposedly conservative English bankers, principally Baring Brothers Bank of London, to put up lots of money to fund The American Association, a company that would build 'A Magic City.' The premise was that what he described as 'vast resources of coal, iron and timber, easily linked by railroad to cities and ports in the East,' would spark a giant industry, similar to what had occurred in Pittsburgh, and was occurring just then in Birmingham, Alabama. 'If you get in on the ground floor, you will be rich; those who wait behind will get nothing.'

Unfortunately, it turned out that there was, and is, little iron ore, and most valuable timber was gone within a few decades; the legacy of coal is mostly destruction…of the environment, and of humans.

Arthur named his city Middlesborough, and assigned names to the broad avenues and streets he laid out, names designed to appeal to bankers from the Midlands of England, who jumped in with Barings. To appeal even more to his English backers, he built a golf course, the second one in the United States. Arthur had the same land-hunger as the aristocracy of colonial Virginia. They got wealthy by giving each other vast grants of land on the unknown side of The Blue Ridge. Arthur's approach, a flimflam of banks, was different in method but not motive.

Arthur used the legend of Cumberland Gap to his advantage. His word pictures flattered English vanity about 'their' colonists. He fed their fantasies with his account of the great cleft in the soaring limestone wall of Cumberland Mountain.

Athiamiowee, The Warriors Path, had been worn smooth by Cherokee and Shawnee hunters and war parties. Long Hunters were the first whites to venture through The Gap, at the head of a long parade: Dr. Thomas Walker in 1750; scores of tough axe men clearing Boone's Trace, a pack-horse trail for Henderson's Transylvania scheme, another land-grab; then hundreds of thousands of settlers. The first critical passageway along The Wilderness Road was the famous Gap at Cumberland Mountain; the second, the water Gap through Pine Mountain (The Narrows); the third, an easy fording-place, which enabled settlers to cross the river and head north toward fertile farmland in the Bluegrass.

'The Magic City' itself was ideally situated, Arthur said: Yellow Creek provided a reliable supply of water, and Yellow Creek Valley, a depression six miles in diameter, the result of the impact of a meteor, made for a broad expanse of land, 'encircled,' as Arthur put it, 'by immense mineral and timber wealth, yet flat as a pancake and easy to settle.'

Arthur's florid prose exceeded even the hyperbolic Victorian standard: 'She is a child of the mountains, with the roses of health upon her cheek, bursting forth into beautiful womanhood to be crowned the

Queen of the Southland; her breath is the pure mountain air that wafts its sweetness throughout the valley, her blushes are the flowers that deck her hillsides, her laughter is the rippling of the streams that gurgle from mountain glens, her jewels are the coal and iron that cluster around her in boundless quantities, her muscles and sinews are the brains and willing and skillful hands of 4,000 good, law-abiding, moral people, while the foundation upon which she stands, firm as the Rock of Gibraltar, is the untold wealth of all her surroundings and possessions.'

Building A Magic City from scratch required imported laborers to construct buildings, dredge the swampy land around Yellow Creek, change the course of the Creek and dam it to create a reservoir at Fern Lake, lay sidewalks, dig and lay the sewer and water system, construct a railroad tunnel under Cumberland Gap, lay over sixty miles of rails to connect the new city with Knoxville, and build a Belt-Line railroad around the city to provide access to coal deposits and mining camps.

The laborers were single footloose young men; many carried a revolver, a knife, or both. The town was thick with bars [one of the first industries was a brewery], gambling dens, and bawdy houses open day and night. Despite Arthur's prose, a boomtown does not attract only 'good, law-abiding, moral people.' The early years saw almost-daily gun battles and knife duels.

Louise was born in the house her father, William Alexander Cooke [W.A.], had built only the year before on Exeter Avenue in an area known as Maxwellton Braes. [The house was still standing in 1995.] W.A.'s father was from Louisa County, Virginia, but moved to Shelbyville in the northern part of Kentucky in 1859, and the next year married Virginia Castleman Jesse, the daughter of Mary Neal.

A hundred years later, Virginia Jesse's great-great-granddaughter traced the family tree to reveal the skein of linkages (physicians at the National Institutes of Health called it 'The Cooke-Jesse Syndrome'), of a gene causing demineralization of the hip socket, and pain and difficulty in walking for many, including my Mother, her sister Ann, several of

Virginia's children and other relations, all of whom had the joint replaced. Today, Americans are living longer, which makes this condition more common; the ball-and-socket simply wear out over time.

In 1890, W.A., his mother and father, and his sister Kate and brother Charles, moved as a family from Shelbyville to Middlesborough to get in on the prosperity. W.A. had been a railway mail clerk in Kansas at a time when the trains were often delayed by herds of buffalo. [When I was a boy and we were living in Wallsend, Louise would send me out to play with a buffalo horn, a souvenir from her father's youth.] W.A., born in 1863, was only twenty-seven in 1890 when he became postal clerk, and then assistant Postmaster, of the new town. He was a reliable Democrat, and President Grover Cleveland appointed him Postmaster in 1893. In 1898 W.A. and Charles opened Cooke Brothers Grocery on Cumberland Avenue, the broad main street with a railroad track running down its middle. W.A. ran the business alone after Charles was appointed Postmaster.

I never met Louise's Uncle Charlie, who in the early '20's went to Lexington to work as an employee at the Odd Fellows headquarters there. But Louise and Dick and I would sometimes visit Charlie's son Allen, her cousin. Allen ran a photography studio in Middlesborough, but was better known for his Houdini act at circuses and carnivals. He billed himself as 'The Human Cork': bound in handcuffs and straightjacket, he would be tossed into the deepest end of a swimming pool or lake. He always escaped and never drowned. I wish I had seen that! And I wish I knew the trick!

Allen married Ada Dozier of Wallins Creek in Harlan County; they had two daughters, Martha and Mildred. (It was Mildred, limping and in pain, who traced out the genetic defect.) I had no way of knowing it when we visited them in the mid-1930s, but Ada would become, only ten years later, almost literally my savior. I OWE HER SO MUCH, and I wish I could tell her face-to-face. But she is dead, as is her husband and both of her daughters. I hope I had the wit to *THANK* her…while I still could!

W.A. was active in real estate, opened a second store, and also operated a farm and a slaughterhouse. In 1904, his store introduced Coca-Cola to Middlesborough. He was a teetotaler, an uncommon attitude in those wide-open boom years. W.A. also held elected office with The Elks Lodge. A photo portrait taken about this time shows a good-looking gentleman, perhaps thirty-five years old, in a well-cut suit, celluloid wing collar and polka dot bowtie, sporting a neatly waxed handlebar mustache.

In 1902 he married a comely 20-year-old redhead from Blythewood, South Carolina, Mayme Dorthula Sloat, whom he had met when she came into the flower shop he ran as a sideline. They began married life in an apartment above the A.D. Campbell Store at 21st and Cumberland Avenue. Their daughter Virginia was born in 1903, twins Rachel and Ralph in 1906, Louise in 1908. The youngest, Angie Sue (Ann), was born in 1909, a few months after her father's death.

W.A. had been bitten in late November by a hog, perhaps one he was trying to slaughter; the wound became infected. He 'lingered,' as Louise described it, for a month, dying on Christmas Eve 1908 of septicemia, more commonly known as blood poisoning. Louise was not quite a year old. She told me that her earliest memory was of her mother's screams of shock and sorrow at her father's death. I wondered then, I wonder now, whether there was some kind of Victorian-era expectation that widows must cry at such-and-such a decibel level, a kind of Vocal Suttee; anything less was an unspoken indictment: They Didn't Really Love Each Other. Whatever the motivation for making grief so public and obvious, Louise was the impressionable young audience for it. She remembered, and told me, of a long period, which in her recollection seemed NEVER to go away, of her mother's choking sobs, her Mother's intense 'agony' of loss and depression.

Her father's obituary said, 'He has always been held in high esteem by his fellow-citizens and has several times held positions of trust and responsibility. He was an ardent, faithful member of the Christian Church, and an active Odd Fellow. He leaves a record of honesty, integrity and worth, as the heritage of his family.' My maternal grandfather died twenty years before I was born. His premature death made a huge difference in my Mother's life, and mine.

This was a time of great stress and grief for a young mother with five very young children. W.A. owned property and several businesses; the widow and orphans should have been reasonably well off. But as Louise remembered it, and as she was told, her young bereaved Mother was a 'taken advantage of' by her husband's supposed friends…in reality, thieves. They offered, ostensibly, to help her manage W.A.'s business affairs, but tricked her and stole everything of value. Within a few years, the estate evaporated to nothing and the family was in desperate straits. Louise was sent to live with her Aunt Kate, who by this time had given up on the so-called boom in Middlesborough and had returned to Shelbyville, where she married.

Louise remembered this period in her life—she was with Aunt Kate and her husband from six to sixteen—as unremitting hardship and labor. She told me, and it was so often repeated it became her Rosary of Despair, how she was 'treated like a servant,' given the most demanding tasks, made to do heavy farm chores in all weather, even bone-freezing cold 'when the skin would come off my hands when I tried to pump water or build a fire.' Louise (though not so far as I know, her siblings) viewed these years through her lifelong perspective of victimization and suffering. Her Father's death, the thieves who bilked her innocent and credulous Mother, the contempt and cruelty of her Aunt Kate, 'as young as I was,' all this was unfair, unjust.

Virginia (d. 1981) married B.F. Barton, who had little education but was thought to be a good farmer. The couple and their growing family moved to Milford, Michigan in the early 1930's. I visited them there several times in 1941 when I lived for a year in Detroit with Ralph and Anne. The Barton family was living a hand-to-mouth hardscrabble existence. I remember Virginia as imbued with the qualities we associate with pioneer women: dour, stoic, uncomplaining…despite grinding deprivation and poverty; she conjures up a vision of Ma Joad in *Grapes of Wrath*. She must have passed on this ethic of work and endurance to her children, who all did well. The eldest joined the Navy, which gave him The G.I. Bill and made it possible for him to earn a doctorate in electrical engineering, which he taught for four decades at the University of Michigan.

Rachel (d. 1956) graduated from Fugazy Business College in Lexington, and was Postmaster (1927-31) in Kenvir (usually called Black Mountain), a new mining camp in Harlan County opened by The Peabody Coal Corporation. She was energetic, popular, full of fun, known to all as 'Cookie' [a nickname derived from a novelty song, 'Lookie, Lookie, Lookie! Here Comes Cookie!,' a hit of the time]. She married William Kusch, comptroller and later superintendent of the big coal operation there. His parents were immigrants from Germany and had worked for Peabody Coal in southern Illinois.

Uncle Bill spoke German and enjoyed playing jokes on me with the language, teaching me the proper pronunciation of foul oaths; he had the stern manner we associate stereotypically and probably unfairly, to Prussians. They had no children, but in 1933 adopted Ken ('Buddy'), one of Virginia's six. When Mayme became seriously ill, Rachel brought her mother from Middlesborough and cared for her. Mayme was the only grandparent I ever saw, but I can't say I truly 'saw' her. In 1935 I was barely six, and she was desperately ill, unspeaking, unmoving, in a room with a spooky quiet hush, curtains drawn. I was told she had 'sleeping sickness.' I still have no idea what caused her death that same year.

I spent quite a bit of time at Black Mountain, partly I suspect because Rachel thought, accurately, that I needed some 'respite' from Judge's drunkenness. Buddy and I enjoyed rolling down their grassy front yard, hunting for crawdads under rocks in the tiny creek across the road, and climbing to the top of the spur across from the houses in 'Official Hollow.' From the spur, we often walked to an enormous man-made mountain, a huge heap of slag and slate, which some years earlier had began to burn, ignited by spontaneous combustion, constantly spewing sulfurous smoke. We walked all over the heap. This was dangerous, because we could feel the heat burning our feet right through our shoes. Had we broken through the crust into one of the glowing red hot spots, we could have been quickly burned to death. Kids have no sense!

My Mom and I had gone to Black Mountain because Rachel had managed to get her into the hospital there for 'the delivery.' That is where my brother Richard Keith Burns was born, January 1935. Dick was often sick as a baby and throughout childhood. He was also very slightly built, though he played football, known affectionately to his teammates as 'Bearcat Burns.' Like me, he was a bookworm, and after he completed college at Morehead State in the north of Kentucky, went on to obtain a Master's in Library Science, an intelligent choice of profession for him.

After graduation, he got a job at The Louisville Public Library, and married a fellow-Librarian there, Frances Forgione. They had two children, dark-haired Judge, who has a lovely daughter Hannah, and red-haired Nina, who has three wonderful children, Max, Frank, and Joseph. Dick then got a much bigger job as Director of the thriving and exceptional Public Library in Falls Church, a well-to-do suburb of Washington. Unfortunately, he contracted tuberculosis, and, as a person in daily contact with the public, the City Fathers required him to treat it so he would not be infectious. This didn't work, and he went to a sanitarium for six months or so, but the disease hung on. He finally opted to have the diseased lung removed by surgery.

The operation was a physical setback. A year or so later, while at a meeting of librarians in Los Angeles, a hemorrhaging ulcer required removal of part of his stomach, another severe health setback. Despite chronic ailments, Dick nonetheless enjoys life. He is partner in a business providing material to folklore specialists all over the world, and has written thousands of reviews of books and recordings in this field.

Rachel and Bill helped Louise and her two kids in many ways. My visits to their home, by comparison with our own situation...our family lurching from crisis to crisis...seemed like an escape to paradise. It was in fact SO MUCH like paradise, that at age nine I set out at six a.m. on a Sunday morning to WALK the sixty miles to that wonderful place; I had walked forty miles, when, several hours after nightfall, a police car pulled up beside me and brought me back to Pineville, exhausted, to confront my Mother's tears.

Rachel was given to snap assessments and instant judgments, instantly verbalized. I think she tried, but was never able, to empathize fully with Louise and her plight. Given Rachel's high-strung nervous energy, it was not a complete surprise when she died of a stroke while chopping down a paw-paw tree in her backyard.

Ralph (d. 1965), an eighth-grade dropout, roared off in 1929 to 'DEE-troit' on his Indian motorcycle. He got a job with Chevrolet Gear and Axle, where he worked for the next 30 years, retiring as soon as he could. He married Anne Turek, whose parents were recent immigrants from Slovakia; she herself, with almost no education, spoke English with a heavy accent. They had no children. But in order to help Louise, struggling hard but not really managing to provide for herself OR her kids after Judge was fired from his Railway Express job, they brought me back, age twelve, to their apartment at 60 N. Clairmont Street in Detroit. I sold *The Detroit Free Press* on the corner of Clairmont and Woodward Avenue (though I was several times beaten up and chased off that corner by other newsboys). The newspapers generated pocket change to pay for Saturday matinees at The Alhambra Theatre. I attended a pretty fair junior high school, and I went every single day to the Branch Library only two blocks away, returning to the apartment carrying huge armloads of books. During the nine months I was there, I worked my way through every volume I could decipher.

Ralph was a fervent supporter of the United Auto Workers, and saw the Union as 'the little guy's only defense' against the power and greed of Big Business. In the late 1930s and increasingly during the War, Detroit was where blacks and whites, both groups mainly from the South and both groups barely educated, confronted each other. The result was a series of ugly race riots. Ralph railed against 'niggers,' and could be relied upon to speak with bitterness and hatred. This was in character for him, as he had a crabbed view of most things. He relished the misfortune of others, but otherwise got little enjoyment from life. As I remember him and his view of the world and all people and things in it, I regret to say that the picture that comes to mind is of a vulgar oaf, both stupid and mean. Ralph didn't think very highly of me, either!

I returned from Detroit when the school year was finished, but Louise was still not able to support her two kids, and, working long hours at The Bakery, was often not even sure where we WERE. She simply had to do SOMEthing. I don't know how she managed it, but in 1942 she somehow got me into Red Bird Settlement School, located in the most remote part of northern Bell County, accessible at that time only by horse or mule, located just over the line from Clay County, infamous for its 'Wars' in which about 150 people were murdered or hanged; it remains one of the poorest counties in the United States. The U.S. Public Health Service supplied the first modern medicine to the most remote hollers. We often saw the 'Nurses On Horseback' around Courthouse Square, their horses loaded with heavy saddlebags of medicine and supplies.

Red Bird had the enormous advantage of being a boarding school; Louise knew that at least I would get supervision and regular food. Best of all, it was FREE!, 'A Mission to the Mountains' of The Evangelical Brethren, a 'Pennsylvania Dutch' sect which later merged with The

Methodists; the Principal's name was Bergstresser, and there were many other 'Deutsch' names.

The driver of the truck carrying the weekly mail run from Pineville lived next door to the Nehi bottling plant, two doors down from the Bakery; this proximity may be how Louise made the connection. He agreed to carry me as a passenger. His pick-up truck, a small Chevrolet, was the first motor vehicle to make it. I'm still amazed…no road, just a horse-trail, but he somehow negotiated the steep and increasingly narrow creek-bed up Stoney Fork to the crest of the mountain, the same route followed in 1945 by the cog railroad used by the W.M. Ritter Lumber Company to carry logs to their mill. On one side of the mountain, water flowed south toward the Cumberland; just over the ridge, water flowed north toward the Kentucky River.

It is obligatory in Bell County, and for that matter everywhere in Appalachia, when first meeting someone, to enquire if you and the stranger might be related, and if so, how? That happened my first day at Red Bird when I wandered into the tiny shack that served as General Store for the remote settlement. Millard Knuckles owned the store, and within a few minutes determined that we were 'cousins,' presumably through my grandmother, Nancy Knuckles.

Cousin or not, that first encounter scared me to death. 'Uncle Millard' kept a Chow-Chow dog, a somewhat exotic breed today; but positively weird to find one so far back in the woods. I had been in the store no more than ten minutes before his dog imagined I did some fool thing that deeply offended his canine sensibilities…and he lunged, biting a sizeable hunk out of my leg. He would have made it all the way to bone if Uncle Millard hadn't beat him off, all the while laughing like a hyena at such an enjoyable respite from his humdrum routine. I continued to patronize the little General Store, and Uncle Millard continued to call me Cousin. Today, I cross the street if I see a Chow coming down the sidewalk.

The Red Bird students were all backwoods kids, tough as hickory. I was completely out of place and had no business at all being there, a scrawny, timid nerd, my nose constantly in a book, totally bereft of farming or mountain skills. Red Bird required that we all work, the girls cooking, cleaning, washing clothes; the boys feeding and milking cows, slopping hogs, cleaning the stable, chopping wood. I was handed a sledgehammer and sent out every afternoon with the other boys; our job was to bust up enough rocks to transform a horse-trail into the semblance of a road. I also had to pitch in with other chores and with building maintenance, the latter leading to a big gash in my thumb, sewn up at the Hospital without benefit of Novocain.

I thank God! it was not me that had to shoot the hog! But I WAS required to pitch in with skinning, butchering, and boiling fat for lard. These were tasks mountain kids knew how to do well, and they loved it. For me, it was hell. The nearest equivalent would be to take Casper Milquetoast and dump him DIRECTLY into Navy Seal training.

Ralph's sister Ann (d. 1982) joined him in Detroit, where for ten years she clerked in the glove department of J.L. Hudson's department store. In 1942 she married Robert Shultz. Ann was intelligent and feminine, with a strong penchant for 'nice things.' I think Bob was attracted to that, aspects of life he knew little of, having been raised in an orphan's home. During Prohibition in the 1920s and early 1930s, he had been a driver and collector [he called it 'enforcer'] for bootleggers ferrying booze across frozen lakes from Canada. He enjoyed talking about those days and seemed to glory in his gangster image. In reality, he was a softie, even though he continued to carry a handgun in a holster under his arm. After Prohibition and up to World War II, he was a male nurse in an upscale insane asylum for the deranged offspring of wealthy families, assigned because of his strength and fearlessness to the most dangerous and unpredictable cases. His main job was to take the men into the woods, where they would unleash their anger by chopping down trees. Bob said he never turned his back when his bunch had axes in their hands.

Bob was likeable, hard working, and confident enough to follow his instincts. The War brought good jobs and good pay. He saw instantly that this was a way to get ahead: he wanted a house, and he wanted to run his own business. He put in double shifts as a welder in the Willow Run tank factory. He was paid on a piecework basis, and given his strength and energy, was able to keep going after others dropped from fatigue. But it was worth it: he was making big bucks, and saving a lot. After the War, he and Ann built their house in the new suburb of Royal Oak, and worked steadily and purposefully to build a thriving dry-cleaning and costume-rental business, as well as a substantial real estate portfolio. Ralph and Anne, who had moved to the same street in the same suburb, just a few doors away, always predicted disaster. Despite his urging, Ralph never went in with any of Bob's investments, all of which made money.

In 1924, Louise returned from Aunt Kate's in Shelbyville. She graduated from Middlesborough High School, and in 1927 obtained a degree in business studies from Lincoln Memorial University in Harrogate, Tennessee, just over the Gap. (One of her classmates was Jesse Stuart, who became one of Kentucky's best-known writers; Louise told me she was sure he had eyes for her.) She was nineteen and just finishing her studies at LMU when she began to notice The Boys From Pineville in their noisy Model Ts, some with rumble seats, roaring over the exceedingly dangerous road around Rocky Face Cliffs, to court the girls in Middlesborough…as many still do. Among them was a young man, well educated and obviously intelligent. Though only twenty-seven, he already had ten years' seniority at a good job. He seemed gentle and kind. He asked her to marry him, and she said yes.

Louise felt that with her father's death, her mother's inconsolable grief, and the theft by confidence-tricksters of every bit of her father's wealth, her life began in tragedy. That is true, and it was surely a difficult beginning. Even sadder is that, for her, suffering seemed never to end.

She was an intelligent and hard-working mother. She did the very best she knew how for her two kids. Despite poverty and a marriage characterized by intermittent abuse, constant chaos, and crushing debts due principally to Judge's alcoholism, she managed a pretty fair job of it.

Louise was diagnosed with heart disease in the 1940's. Physicians warned her that she risked sudden death; she must quit work *immediately*. She outlived every one of those physicians, dying fifty years later of congestive heart failure. Her ashes are now a part of The Dr. Thomas Walker Historic Site, a knob that provides a spectacular view through The Narrows, with lots of flowering dogwood and soft pink mountain laurel in May. I hope Louise is able to rest there comfortably, close to what she always thought of as 'home.' My brother Dick and I thought this better than a conventional grave, our mother pinned to earth by a heavy granite headstone.

IMAGINARY ANCESTORS, 1747–1935

◆

I do not know how my father's family, nor or my mother's, came to America. They, like most, were probably illiterate. There are no early records at all, and it seems impossible we could ever really know. They were 'bound and determined' to create a better life; grit and perseverance enabled most to achieve their goal. Judge was 'Scotch-Irish'...Louise, English. The four accounts that follow are entirely IMAGINARY. But the stories are plausible, certainly not impossible. Perhaps our ancestors experienced something like this...

WARD GILLEY (The Hunter) = marries (1756) Sally Sizemore (1747-1791[?])
      children: LILAH GILLEY [found child]
      Mason Gilley [natural child]

      LILAH GILLEY = marries (1773) Simon Begley
          children: MAGGIE BEGLEY, and other children...

HARGIS BROUGHTON (The Settler)
      = marries (1778) MAYME TOLBERT (d. 1781), d. of FRASER T.
      one child:

ROBERT BROUGHTON (The Miller)
(1779-1845)

HARGIS BROUGHTON (The Settler)
= marries (1781) MAGGIE BEGLEY
children: James Broughton, (1783-1845), other children...

Gilley Broughton, *grandson* of HARGIS B.
(1818-1889)

H.C. (HENRY CLAY) BROUGHTON (The Sawyer)
(1848-1935), *great-grandson* of HARGIS B.

VIRGIL STURGILL, killed 1780 at Battle of King's Mountain

AMBROSE STURGILL (*Tollgate Keeper*), son of Virgil Sturgill

Homer Sturgill, son of Ambrose S. = marries (1807)
Nancy Jackson, d. of CARTER JACKSON (The Planter)
children: Carter Sturgill   (Miller's Apprentice)

THE HUNTER
WARD GILLEY, 1749–1791(?)

◆

James Broughton's grandmother lived with him and his wife Maggie after Simon Begley died in 1798. It was only then that The Old Woman began to tell her story. James did not know Lilah Bagley's age. But her dark pigmentation, high cheekbones and hooked nose revealed her half-Indian ancestry.

'Paw was called 'Ward Gilley' but that warn't his real name and he warn't my real daddy.' Lilah told her tale between puffs on her brown-stained cob pipe.

He was born in Liverpool 'in seventeen an' forty-nine.' His mother died of 'bloody consumption' when the boy was ten; there were no other children. The family lived at the raw edge of existence. Charles' father worked twelve hours a day, with only The Sabbath as A Day of Rest. Charles' mother grew thinner and weaker every day. Soon she could do no housework or even get to the slop jar. When she died, her bones covered by a sheet stained red by her blood, the boy could not understand. He asked, *Why?*

A year later, his father, Noah Netherton, was severely injured when a wagon tipped and a load of paving stones smashed his legs. He was never able to walk again. He borrowed money to buy food, hoping to find work a cripple might do, and repay. But he was never able to find employment. He pleaded for more time. But **The Law is The Law.** He was sent to Debtor's Prison. His son Charles was eleven. On the three occasions he was permitted to visit, Charles tried to be cheerful, but there was little to say. Had his father been fit for fieldwork, The Crown would have sent him, Indentured, to The Virginia Plantations. But as a cripple, he could only make brooms, and wait for death. Charles' bitterness grew.

The boy spent the next two years on the streets, lurking in the shadows, dodging footpads, sleeping under bridges and stairs. It was a life of constant fear, lived in a nauseous hellhole of drunkenness and prostitution, crime and venality. Great hordes of orphans roamed the streets day and night. Because of his terror of the gangs, Charles himself fell in with a group of boys who could run fast and knew where to hide. If nothing else, they could try to protect each other.

They spent most of their time begging. But this usually resulted in hard stares, curses, and sometimes a blow from a crop. As their hunger mounted, they became more desperate. Charles' gang worked together: half the boys would start yelling and fighting each other, raising a loud ruckus. Once attention was diverted, the others would quietly sneak up beside a market stall, and dart out a hand to hide bread under a shirt. Sometimes they picked pockets or cut purses. They lived by grabbing what they could, by any means they could.

A few months later, Charles and two other boys began working with The Rat Catcher. Charles was slim and able to slide under the foundations of houses. His job was to set out traps and poisons, then a day later slip back under the house to remove dead rats before the rotten stink began to seep up through the floorboards. It was not a job he would have chosen…but he had No Choices.

The Rat Catcher also hired Charles and his gang to supply the main attraction for the rat pits. They went out at night to the open garbage dumps found on every corner. The boys used tongs to catch the rats, and burlap bags to hold them. The Rat Catcher paid a farthing for every one he deemed 'lively.'

The rat pits were the best entertainment in The City...except for hangings. Nothing could beat a good hanging. Charles' gang never missed one, since a hanging meant easy pickin's. Several thousand people crowded as close to the gallows as they could manage, packed in so close there was no way to move. The strongest elbowed their way to the front, as close as they could get to the hanged man's face (but sometime it was a woman).

Seeing the face was the best part. The hangings were a wonderful diversion. But for pickpockets, a hanging was not an entertaining spectacle, but a profitable enterprise. The crowd was dense, their attention transfixed on the snap! of the rope and the dying man's last gasp. Sometimes the victim would dance in the air, and when the black hood was removed, his face was purple and his tongue protruded. The crowd loved every bit of it. For experienced pickpockets, and by this time the gang had much experience, there could not possibly be a better occasion than a good hanging to sneak in a hand and steal. They made good money off hangings.

The only hanging when his gang came away with little was when one of their own, Bowser (they thought he was ten), was hanged after he was caught stealing bread. Mothers, and even a few men, wept, and there was much muttering: 'What an unfortunate creature! What an innocent sweet face! I might steal myself if'n I was starving! To think! To kill a boy so young! But he WILL go to Heaven, for sure. Won't he? Ain't he SURE to go STRAIGHT to Heaven!'

All cried and wailed, giving vent to strong, sincere sentiment. Still, they were impatient for the entertainment to begin. All understood. All shook their heads solemnly. All intoned, 'The Law is The Law.'

His chum Bowser had shared his bread, and Charles simply could not look. 'If The Assize says 'Hang 'im 'cause he's hungry an' stole bread,' then Th' Judge can kiss my ass.' Charles' hatred of Laws and Constables and Judges started when his father went to Debtor's Prison. His fierce anger grew so strong it seemed to consume him. The way he saw it, the world was animated by cruelty. Nobody cared one good Goddamn about him or about anybody but themselves, and he felt precisely the same toward them. But his was a *quiet* hatred. This fire burned within. *He had to be tough to survive, and he was determined to survive.* His hatred, of both God and Law, deepened when Bowser was hanged for stealing bread. Even after he grew to be a man, Charles never changed his opinion.

The rat pits were four feet deep, circular, sides covered with zinc or tin so the animals could not claw their way out. When enough people had paid the admission and assembled at the pit, and when enough bottles of cheap Barbados rum had been sold and consumed, it was time to bring in, to the lusty cheers of the drunken crowd, The Rat Catcher And His Boys with their writhing bags.

It was necessary to carefully enumerate the rats in the pit, as the betting depended on the number killed, and the number still left alive at the end, usually none at all. The boys dangled each rat by its tail as The Pit Boss kept a tally. The spectators cheered every time a squirming rat was dropped in. Soon the pit was a swarm…precisely one hundred rats…rats scrambling, rats crawling over each other, rats running round and round the pit aimlessly, rats with no escape.

The drunken cheers grew louder when The Dogs were brought in. Charles thought they were some kind of terrier. Whatever kind they might be, they were fast and fearless. The most famous was Black Jack, his muzzle deeply scarred by numerous rat bites from many previous encounters. When this Champion Dog was carried in, straining every muscle to leap out of his owner's arms and into the rat pit, the roar was deafening. Intermingled amongst the men were a few whores, painted faces and leering smiles, some brazenly grabbing a spectator's crotch, anything to stir a little interest, drum up some business. The men reeled drunkenly, cursed, boasted, yelling out side bets. Most bet against The Pit Boss.

The Boss knew his dogs, and he knew what they could do. This was business, and he had no intention whatsoever of losing money at business. 'Place your bets, gentlemen: Ten bob for five if Black Jack don't snap ten in five minutes. A guinea for ten bob if he don't snap all hund'rd in thirty minutes.'

Rat catching was a good job. Charles had no fear at all of rats, though he was bitten many times, and was often covered with fleas. But he was terrified of The Rat Catcher, who enjoyed nothing better than slapping his gang of boys. He laughed when he banged them so hard their heads smacked against the pavement, or when he pushed them into the open sewers that ran down the middle of the cobblestones. He laughed if they screamed when he kicked them.

Then a better job came along. For weeks Charles had hung around a blacksmith shop in The Chandler's Yard at the north end of the port. The Smith cursed like a sailor, not surprising since his clients were in fact sailors charged with supplying and fitting-out the boats. This day the Smith's face was a mask of black anger, his oaths more foul than usual. 'That damn pinhead kid is gone! Claims he kin be a farrier on a farm! He don't know one God'sbod thing about shoeing horses! I hope to CHRIST! he's kicked in the head and DIES!'

The cursing abated for a minute, and the Smith turned to Charles: 'I need a bellows-boy. Five-pence a day.' And for the next eight months, Charles carried in huge bags of charcoal, heavy billets of iron, kept the fires topped up, and pumped the bellows till he thought his arms would drop right off.

The Smith had more work than he could handle, and was working long and hard to keep up. Liverpool Captains were in a frenzy to cash in on the slave-rum trade, fitting out any kind of boat they thought might be seaworthy enough to make the voyage. But a blacksmith was essential. The Captains needed hundreds of iron neck nooses, and double that number of ankle clasps. Some specified nooses and clasps linked by iron chains, others specified that the shackles be linked by long iron bars for a coffle. The Smith had no opinion on the matter. He would forge iron any way The Captains wanted. Just as long as they paid. Cash.

The Smith made good money supplying iron shackles, but absolutely would NOT board the boats to bolt them in. He had done this *once*, two decks down on a ship just back from The Indies. The Smith looked strong as an ox, and nearly was. Nor was he fainthearted. But the odor was overpowering. This airless black hole was like the foulest depth of a cesspit. He inhaled the powerful reek of vomit-sweat-shit-piss, the most nauseating stench he had ever experienced. He staggered up on deck, choking, gasping for air. 'KEEP your ten guineas! Your Carpenter can do this rotten job!' The Captain replied, 'Have mercy, my good man! *Think how hard it is on US!* 'Tis very hard indeed! These Africans is nasty by Nature. All of 'em stink like a ten-day corpse! This ain't no Trade for them with tender noses!'

Charles watched and learned. After a month or so, the blacksmith gave him pincers and let him hold bars in place while the Smith hammered at the anvil. Charles was starting to think he knew a little something. But he changed his mind in an instant when he got a horrible burn; a piece of red-hot iron leapt off the anvil and landed on his foot. The boy screamed, then bit his tongue. He walked with a slight limp from that time onward. But he didn't quit. Within a few minutes he hobbled back to the bellows-bag, pumping to make the coals as hot as the Smith wanted. He was determined to hang on, and learn. A searing burn and an ugly scar and a little limp were nothing…if he could learn a trade.

Then…a sudden Change Of Fortune.

Chandler Yard loomed black in the December night. Charles waited for the Smith to lock up, and stumbled out the door in the dark toward the stairs under which he slept. As he turned the corner, his arms were pinned, and he was bound tightly with a rope. He knew immediately what had happened; he had heard stories from the other boys, and even scarier stories from sailors in The Yard.

The kid-nabber gang dragged him and nine other boys, all tightly bound with rope, to a boat at the far end of the quay. The kid-nabbers told The Captain they wanted ten pounds apiece. 'Liverpool will be well served, Cap'n, well served indeed, to be quit o' scum like these here pickpockets. Good riddance to bad rubbish, don't ye agree?' But the Captain said the boys were too small. He'd pay fifty pounds for the lot, and that was his Final Offer.

'It was all done proper,' Gilley told his daughter: "Th' gang paid a Bailiff fer *A Paper* saying we was all Orphans, we had no Guardian, that th' Parish was Poor, an' that we was being Transported to Plantations in His Majesty's Colony of Virginia fer Healthful Work, where we would be the Ward of an Overseer. Th' Captain demanded Th' Paper before he'd let us boys on board."

Lilah looked straight at her grandson. 'My Paw hated Paper, hated to be FORCED to do things, hated Laws, hated Rules, hated Trickery most of all. I can hear his words in my ear right now: "That Bailiff's Paper sold me into slavery! That's why I hate Paper. Them words is LIES! Every word on Paper is A LIE. I wouldn't wipe my ass on Paper!"

When they docked...the human cargo...thirteen Indentured Voluntaries, ten Orphans, and eight Convicts...were paraded on deck by the Captain, then auctioned off like cattle to the highest bidder. A Soul Driver bought Lilah's father and nine other boys, paying The Captain twenty pounds each.

Not as good as some voyages, The Captain thought. Still, not too bad: Four times what I paid per head in Liverpool.

As Lilah's father told it to her, "Th' Soul Driver had a whip an' was mean as a feist dog. He tied us boys together an' marched us ten days, fed us nothin' but Injun corn an' water. He sold us off to any Plantation along th' road th' minute he could turn a profit off'n us. But me an' another boy was young an' we didn't look too strong, so he kep' drivin' th' two o' us along. Bye an' bye we come to Great Lick in Th' Big Valley. That was where th' Soul Driver had Good Luck and we was Shit Out o' Luck. Three buck slaves had just died o' Flux an' Fever on a 'backer plantation, an' Th' Overseer needed field hands right now if he was a-goin' to git in a crop. Th' Driver signed a Paper an' got sixty pounds fer th' two o' us. I stuck it out fer a year 'til I got th' lay o' th' land. Then I run away…as fer as I could git."

'An' that's how Papaw ended up in Great Lick, an' that's why he always said 'I run away from Virginny.'

Like thousands of others, slaves and indentured servants, the boy headed as far from civilization as his legs would carry him. He was off The Plantation, but his worries were far from over. "Suppose Th' Overseer comes after me? Suppose he puts out word 'bout a runaway field hand name o' Charles Netherton?"

"But s'pose I *warn't* 'Charles Netherton'?'

"My mother's family name was Gilley; that seems good enough. An' th' Bailiff's paper said th' Overseer would care for me as 'A Ward.' *SO BE IT.*'

'Papaw said, 'From time on, *my name was WARD GILLEY.*"

'Paw was proud he was free, proud he could choose his own name, might proud he could pick a name he liked, any name he wanted. He liked his new name. He thought 'Ward Gilley' suited him proper. He 'specially liked that there warn't nobody to tell him what he Had To Do. There warn't No Paper. An' he sure as sartin warn't fixin' to do no farmin'.'

As soon as the boy was well over The Blue Ridge, he came upon six Hunters on horseback, a train of eight packhorses behind them. 'They set off toward the west. Paw just ran along behind, an' they din't seem to mind. Paw din't have airy idea whar they was headed, but so long as it warn't toward The Plantation, he din't much care. If'n he din't ask fer a horse to ride, an' agreed to do all th' hard work, an' do it quick an' never talk back, an' din't want no money, him an' Th' Hunters got along real good. Paw tole me their names, but the onliest ones I can recollec' now is Walden, Baker, Crockett, an' Cutshaw. Cutshaw war the one Paw talked 'bout th' most. He warn't tall, but he was quick an' strong, an' he knew ever' thing there was to livin' in Th' Wilderness. Paw said it was him that learned him how to track game an' pack out hides.'

'Many o' them that come to Kaintuck later on was skeered. They was skeered o' laurel thickets, skeered o' canebrakes. They was BIG trees everwhar, an' they was skeered o' shadders in th' woods. Maybe an Injun was gonna leap out an' scalp 'em daid. But Papaw was never skeered. He was happy as a pig in slop…no Debtor's Prison, no Rat-Catchers, no lying Bailiffs, no Soul Drivers, no Overseers flailin' skin off'n th' backs o' field hands, white or black.' *The Wilderness was freedom.* Ward Gilley would live off what the forest provided. And since his childhood had taught him to ask for very little and expect even less, the woods amply provided all he needed. *He was never happier than the day he headed into The Wilderness.*

The Hunters, the boy plodding behind, went up an animal trail, a north-south path they said was followed by Cherokee from Carolina and Shawnee from Ohio country. 'Papaw said The Hunters said they was more skeered o' Injuns than o' any kind o' beast. If they saw the Injuns comin', they'd hide an' hope th' Injuns just passed 'em by. But they had their rifles primed and ready. The Hunters dressed pretty much jes' like Injuns 'cept fer linen shirts, some dyed brown as earth from juice o' black walnut hulls. That was what they wore in th' summer. The Injuns wanted horses an' rifles an' would sneak up an' steal 'em, or kill the Hunters an' jes' take 'em. An' o' course the Injuns was Big in the Tribe if they come back with white scalps. Mostly they was out huntin', same as Cutshaw an' all the rest. Aroun' the fire, th' Hunters' allowed as how th' Injuns had as much right to hunt as they did.'

'But in The Wilderness, it was KILL OR BE KILLED! Paw said one time they sneaked up on a gang o' six Shawnee…kilt ever' one an' stole their hides. Then they scalped 'em an' stuck those scalps in their belts jes' like Injuns. It was bloody War…an' not that along ago! Right here, a day's ride from where we're settin'!'

'One o' the Hunters had traded with Injuns an' knew some o' their talk. He was the first to warn 'em all…*You dassn't turn yer back!*' Injuns'll steal yer horse, yer gun, yer hides…then strip ye bare-naked, an' roast ye in a bonfire!'

'Later on, Paw traded with some Cherokee, though he knew he could'a been kilt!…He stayed with 'em 'bout a week, an' learnt some words. They give him an Injun pipe. He smoked hit fer th' longest time 'til one night he was drunk, an' fell an' broke hit. After that he made a bowl out o' a cob, but he kep' th' Injun stem.'

They followed Indian Creek, which led to a high cleft in the mountain, more saddle than Gap. A towering wall of limestone stretched beyond sight to the northeast, and beyond sight to the southwest. When they had climbed to the crest of the saddle, they found a hole in the mountain with a constant breeze of cool air gently blowing out, and a small stream of water gushing from a spring deep inside…sweetest water anywhere. The Hunters called the place Cave Gap.

They followed the trail down the mountain. They kept to the path as it followed a creek, then a few more miles to a big stream that The Hunters said was the Shawnee river. Lilah said 'My Paw said them mountains war' so full of game it war' beyon' belief. But to get to th' most game you had to go through a narrer water Gap. Then they come to a little Hill at th' place where you could wade 'cross th' river. The Hunters told Paw th' Hill was where th' Injuns buried their people. Then high ridges, steep cliffs, big rivers, creeks an' hollers all over, so many you could easy lose your way. Th' Injuns called th' water Gap '*Wasioto*'. Papaw didn't know th' meaning o' th' word, but from there on, a hunter could find more deer an' elk than anywheres else, especially on Th' Bald Knobs, mountain tops th' Injuns had burnt off, an' where they was grass. He guessed maybe that's what th' word meant.'

Gilley and The Hunters spent months in The Wilderness, operating from a Station Camp a day's ride north of a salt lick a few miles beyond The Ford. They kept hunting…until they had accumulated enough tanned hides to make full loads for their horses. A few had 'made their mark' on contracts to supply salt buffalo and venison to feed British soldiers; others had agreed to supply well scraped and cured deerskin and elk hides for export to Europe. In cold weather, they dressed in deerskin leggings, and a long open-front frock also of deerskin, with a cape to shed rain. The frock was tied with a broad leather belt, into which they stuck tomahawk and skinning-knives. Each Hunter slung his powder horn and charger over his shoulder, as well as a pouch for lead shot. Their garments were stained with sweat…and with animal blood and grease, since the essence of the work was to kill as many animals as possible, strip them of their skins, and using a dull draw-knife, scrape off hair and every bit of flesh. Cutshaw's jacket was decorated with dyed porcupine quills, his leggings embellished with fringe. Some Hunters wore caps of 'possum or bear or 'coon fur. Cutshaw wore a broad-brimmed hat of black felt, flagged by two feathers, one white, one red, the crown encircled with blue wampum beads.

They made moccasins from tough elkskin, and Cutshaw made a pair for Gilley. The weather was turning frosty, so he fashioned them with the fur on the inside, padded and warm. Gilley later learned the felt had been carefully prepared by Cutshaw's Indian Old Woman.

The Hunters took as much care of their feet as he did of their rifles. Every night when they camped, they dried their moccasins by the fire, and put their feet so close to the coals Gilley thought they might bake. But Cutshaw warned him that scald feet was serious trouble: Hunters HAD to stay mobile. They slept under rock ledges, or in wigwams of saplings covered with hides or bark. Wool shirts, great coats, and buffalo pelts kept them warm in winter, though the pelts were full of fleas from a pack of dogs, acquired at Stalnaker's. But the dogs were good trackers and barked menacingly at any animals nosing 'round in the dark. One dog was later so badly mauled by a bear, they gave it a merciful death with one shot.

They were gone three months before they headed back with a valuable load of summer deer hides, skins that were thinner and more pliable than deer hides from other seasons. They also brought in a few bear and buffalo pelts. Cutshaw traded his pelts for a brindle mare, blind in one eye but otherwise sound, and a rifle, scarred but serviceable, which he presented to Gilley. The Hunters dispersed, saying they would meet and head out again in two weeks.

Cutshaw bought glossy black French powder, lead bars, and two pecks of meal. He then disappeared. Stalnaker said, 'Cutshaw's off to see 'His Old Woman.' The Trader added nothing more, and the boy didn't dare ask. Gilley slept in the barn. When Cutshaw came riding back, his clothing was less stained, nor did it smell as strong as when they had ridden in. The only thing he said was, 'With another horse, we can pack out more.' The Hunters straggled back one by one. Over the next few days, they traded for powder and shot they expected to need for an indefinite stay in The Wilderness. Then they saddled up and headed off again…westward.

An itinerant Smith came by Stalnaker's every May and October. Cutshaw usually showed up then in case his horses needed shoeing. All of the Hunters had a craftsman's concern for their tools. They wanted every thing necessary for survival, but refused to carry even one extra ounce, though a few permitted themselves a pewter plate and cup. They were obsessive about their rifles, taking them completely apart on a regular schedule. They cleaned the heavy octagonal barrel with linen shooting patches, greased with bear fat. They re-set the angle of the thin clear flint and steel frizzen plate and spring; they cleaned the flash pan, and cleaned out the touch hole with a pin. They greased other parts with tallow, reassembling the rifles good as new…and much cleaner. Several carried hand-vises, and all were adept at repairs…hundreds of miles from a blacksmith.

They used their whetstones every day, and tomahawks and skinning knives stayed razor-sharp. Their knives varied greatly in design, but all were impressive, some more than a foot long. The blades had been re-worked from steel files, some with bone handles incised with elaborate designs. Files were also used in the hawk head of the tomahawks they all carried and which were used many times a day. The head of the hatchet was a kind of sandwich: file-steel in the middle to make a sharp cutting edge, pig iron on both sides for heft. On one trip, Cutshaw asked the Smith to make him a tripod of iron with three S-shaped hooks, so they could suspend meat over the fire. Most of the Hunters carried elkskin bags of Indian trade goods, mirrors, beads, shiny coins…coins of any value…so long as they bore a likeness of The King.

The Hunters went out as a group…on the ancient principle of safety in numbers. But though they were prepared to fight and die together if it came to that, they owned their hides individually. Cutshaw and Gilley occasionally went off alone, but the others considered this so dangerous as to be virtual suicide, as Indians liked nothing better than a lone and therefore defenseless Hunter, easy prey to kill and scalp. Cutshaw and the Hunters went out in all seasons, simply ignoring rain, snow or ice. They were after hides, not like Settlers or Indians who hunted most often in the Fall, seeking fat animals for food. The Hunters preferred new territory, as they had usually shot out almost all the game on earlier forays. In addition, carcasses and bones polluted the forest air with a foul reek that even Cutshaw found repellent. It reminded Gilley of his youth in Liverpool, removing dead rats. The carcasses also attracted packs of wolves, feeding on guts and carrion piled in stinking rotten heaps beside the skinning poles.

The Hunters feared Indians…some regarded them as little better than vermin to be exterminated. Others admired their bravery. All acknowledged that Indians knew more woodcraft, and had much to teach them about surviving in The Wilderness. However, all were con-temptuous of 'Injun speerets. We kill all the game we kin. An' so do they! Do they sleep better? Do they eat better? if'n they ask 'Permission'? SHOOT 'EM! SKIN 'EM!…That's all they is TO it!'

The Hunters needed very little from The Trading Post, but their hides fetched good money, and they had to spend it on something. So when they rode westward into The Wilderness, their saddlebags were full of meal or parched corn, plenty of black powder, lead, tobacco, sometimes oats as a treat for the horses, and, always, big jugs of corn whiskey.

Gilley still wore the coarse linen shirt, the heavily worn and patched wool frockcoat, leather breeches and cloth cap that The Overseer had grudgingly provided. But as the Hunters packed to begin their third trip, Cutshaw tossed him a frock and leggings of deerskin. 'These was sewed by my Old Woman.' Gilley didn't know what to say, so he said nothing. He was proud that at last he looked like A Hunter. Later, he fashioned himself a warm cap from a 'coon he had shot, skinned, and tanned himself. Some of the Hunters never stopped talking…Cutshaw was the opposite: he was not a man of FEW words…he was a man of NO words.

As the months and years went by, Gilley learned the names and qualities of every tree and plant…which were good to eat, which good for medicine…as poultices, or brewed like sassafras tea. They got a bit of honey from hives in hollow gum trees. They usually wouldn't bother if the yellow jackets were swarming, but sometimes had to risk it if they needed beeswax for flux when they melted lead and poured shot. Some lead was re-melted from balls extracted from animals they killed. They gorged on pawpaws or wild strawberries and blackberries when they found them. But their diet consisted essentially of one thing…day-in-day-out, meat and more meat, pounded into pemmican, or, usually, roasted till it was black enough to suit…turkey, elk, deer, buffalo. Sometimes bass or catfish.

Lilah said, 'Papaw liked squirrel th' best, then deer-meat. An' he sure loved b'ar-meat, 'specially in th' fall, when th' b'ars was fat an' tasty as big boar hogs, full up with hickory nuts an' chestnut mast.'

Cutshaw spoke hardly a word. But Gilley watched so intently and copied so minutely, The Hunter began to let the boy do a little hunting. A second rifle was protection for all, since a gut-shot animal had to be dispatched before it could attack. Even so, there were many close encounters with catamounts, bear, buffalo, or with she-wolves defending cubs or feeding on rotting carcasses. Gilley became adept with the priming rod, could gauge the amount of powder for the distance, and could deftly insert wadding and shot. Practice made him accurate...After a time, he never wasted a single ball. He became quick at gutting and at stripping hides with the skinning pole. He was soon producing skins with 'clean cuts.' It took years to become skilled at tracking, but this, too, came eventually. Later, Cutshaw began to entrust him with the more delicate task of cleaning hides and tanning them...mainly in creek beds from a brew of acorns and tanbark. The Hunters made salt by boiling brine at licks. Tanning was important, because if not done properly, the hides fetched hardly enough for powder and shot.

One time at The Trading Post, Cutshaw brought in a baby, obviously half-Indian. The baby crawled around on the rough puncheon floor for an hour or two, then The Hunter rode back with it toward his Old Woman. He never told the baby's name or said whether he had a wife...and Gilley didn't dare ask. But the baby stirred something in Gilley. His life so far had been little but hardship and meanness, and he had silently cursed both God and Law. But this baby was not hard or mean. Was this what preachers meant when they spoke of 'soul,' or of 'Merciful God'? He began to ask himself: is this a possibility?

For four years Gilley hunted with the others, though he was still too young and green to be considered an equal. He often went out with Cutshaw as a two-man team. The boy got paid when Cutshaw sold hides, but not in money. What would he do with money? His pay was a horn all his own, scraped till it was transparent enough to see the black powder, and thus gauge how much was left. Dangling from its end was a powder measure he made from the tip of a deer's horn. On the next trip Gilley was paid with a mold and lead pot, and Gilley made himself a handsome elkskin pouch for them. He longed for a big knife he had seen, and on their fourth trip, Cutshaw gave it to him. Later, when they sold a particularly valuable load, Cutshaw traded the beat-up old rifle Gilley had been using, replacing it with a handsome new one made in Lancaster. It had a Rock Maple stock, curly grain with tiger stripes, artfully incised with an elaborate design. There was a hinged brass box in the stock to hold greased patches. Cutshaw tested it first: truest ball he'd ever fired. Gilley had known little love in his life…but he deeply loved that rifle.

Gilley wondered, Why did they bother with hides at all? The forest supplied their food. For the rest, What did they need, really? A bedroll, a steel striker and yellow flint to make a campfire, but flint could be found all over. With money off hides, the Hunters could buy whisky, and did. And, if so inclined, money could buy women. What money DID provide, was more of what they had ALREADY…the feeling that they were FREE MEN. None of them could abide doing someone else's bidding. They'd rather starve than that…But good hunters never starve.

The years had gone by quickly. Gilley wasn't sure, but he thought he was now about eighteen. He wasn't afraid; he knew what to do. He could make it in the woods on his own. And on his own…ALONE, completely ALONE, dangerous, even foolhardy, as it was…was exactly the way he wanted it.

'Papaw didn't' want nobody, Walden or Baker or Crockett, not even Cutshaw, tellin' him what to do nor when to do it, nor how to do it! He tole me, 'Hell! Maybe I won't do nothin'! It's me that decides. No piece o' paper.'

Cutshaw said that if Gilley was 'bound and determined' to hunt on his own, he HAD to have a better horse. On their next trip in, Cutshaw inspected a sorrel left at The Post for sale. He said it looked 'likely.' He examined its teeth, its hooves, its withers, loaded it with saddlebags full of heavy lead bars, and rode it hard for two hours. He came back and said, 'I think this'un'll do.' He made the boy promise his first load of hides as payment. This seemed Fair Enough.

The stock of his rifle was so richly decorated there was little blank space left. But Gilley found a spot near the cheek piece on which to carve his own Mark...He asked The Factor to write it down, so he had something to copy:

WG
1768

Ward Gilley struck out. For the next twenty years he was a Long Hunter, gone for months at a time...sometimes with groups at Station Camps, sometimes on his own...in remote areas of the dark back-woods...then emerging with huge pack-loads of deer and elk hides, and bison and bear pelts. The bearskins were used by settlers to keep warm. Bear pelts became more valuable when Grenadier units began to use them to decorate their headgear. Later, Gilley trapped beaver and sold their pelts as well. Beaver was in demand to make hats for fashionable gentlemen. He sold at several Posts, but traded most at the Post where Cutshaw had first taken him...Stalnaker's, between The Forks of The Holston, so well known it was indicated on maps by 1750. His grand-mother Lilah told James that her father's pelts fetched the best price cause he knew th' Injun' way o' tannin'.

James tried to calculate when all this happened, but since he couldn't read or write or count much, he wasn't able to get very far. For one thing, he didn't know when his grandmother Lilah was born. He did remember that she was wrinkled up an' bent over, her voice like a hen cackle, an' didn't have airy tooth in her haid. Would that have been in 17 an' 98? An' did that mean Ward Gilley landed in Virginny in 17 an' 62? Who knew? Did it matter? They didn't have a Bible and nobody knew how to write, had there been a Bible.

Lilah told James, 'My Paw loved squirrel. He could live fer weeks on nothin' but squirrel. Though, if he had it, he'd boil up some hominy or meal, or he'd chew on jerky. An' later on, he liked fried hog meat, when we had some.'

When she was a young girl, Lilah was fascinated by her father's stories. 'He was always puffin' on a pipe, sometimes chewin' 'backer an' puffin' all at oncet. An' he shore did like his jug. He pulled on his jug till he couldn't stand up, but th' more he sucked on th' jug, th' longer he talked. He'd talk till he jes' went to sleep. Hit was a sight if he pulled on his jug, but swallowed his chaw instead. We'd like to died a-laughin'. Papaw'd stretch out on th' cabin porch, layin' on a long canvas croker sack o' corn shucks. An' talk! He'd talk till th' sun went down!'

'Th' hunt he 'membered most clear, th' one he'd tell hit…over an' over…was when he was near kilt, but not by a b'ar.' Gilley had been hunting on his own maybe five years, though he "couldn't right recollec." On this trip, he'd been in the woods four months and had two horse-loads ready to pack out, when he discovered fresh bison scat. He determined he'd come out with one more pelt.

'So he piled rocks on his hides an' stacked rocks all 'round, so no animal could get at 'em whilst he was out huntin' the buffalo. He spent all-of-a-day trackin', till he spied seven of' 'em feedin' on cane, three cows, three calves, an' a big ol' bull, biggest my pappy ever seed. He shot it oncet, an' he knew th' ball hit.'

'But th' bull kep' on, straight fer 'im. Papaw took off, primin' his rifle on th' run. He got off one more shot, which hit th' beast in his haid. Th' bull just dropped…plumb daid on th' spot, right at Papaw's feet. Well, he made a fire an' feasted right thar on th' bull's tongue. Next mornin' he skinned hit, loaded that heavy ol' skin on one o' his horses, so he could git hit to his cache. He figgered to lug it over to Greasy Creek, an' then tan it proper.'

'He was 'bout hailing distance from his rock shelter when he heard a horse. Like a whinny? Well, Papaw tied up his two horses, primed his rifle, an' went quiet as anything through th' soft ground to where he could see. He spied three horses tied up 'side his cache, rocks all throwed off. He saw a man with a dirty face an' a long beard. Papaw saw he was a white man all right, an' as ugly as th' Rat-Catcher…loadin' his hides onto two o' th' horses.'

'Papaw aimed.'

"STOP RIGHT THERE! THEM HIDES IS MINE!"

'Th' varmint came at him right off, a tomahawk way up over his head. Pappaw said he thought he'd be brained fer sartin. He rolled down a long hill, an' whilst he was a-rollin', grabbed out his skinnin' knife. Th' varmint leapt agin. Paw moved quick so th' man couldn't get him, an' just as he did, he put his knife into that varmint's belly, right up to th' handle. Papaw BRAGGED on it. He never LET UP braggin' on it! 'Ain't nothin' wrong with killin' a man what's stealin' yer hides!'

'But jes' then, he heard twigs a-snappin'. He crawled back up th' hill, jes' as an' Injun was makin' off with th' horses an' his hides. They had a good start on him, an' Paw had to run to catch up. He yelled, an' fired. Th' Injun fell an' never moved. Paw went up to look, but he had his tomahawk out to use if'n he had to.'

'Well, he near fell down when he seed th' Injun war' a woman! Her face was so sooty with black smoke, you couldn't hardly make out her color. But she had a nose an' face like an Injun, an' skin like an Injun. He thought this woman was Cherokee…but not dressed like any Cherokee he'd ever seed before.'

'An' she war daid!"

'Then Paw fetched their horses, two with his hides, one with a saddle an' bags behind. An' there inside one o' them bags…war an Injun papoose on a cradle-board! It war whimperin', but it warn't hurt none.

Paw said he din't have airy idea, no idea a-tall, what to do. He warn't 'shamed o' killin' them varmints. 'Them sum-bitches was stealin' my hides, an' one tried to scalp me. Of COURSE I kilt 'em!"

'Well, you know THAT BABY WAS ME. Papaw said he thought maybe he'd just leave th' baby there. What could he do with a baby? What good would a baby be? He had no use fer a baby! But he picked hit up an' looked at hit: its skin was not plain Injun. Was th' dead varmint the daddy? He inspected th' creature, like he might look over a beast he'd never seed before…It 'peared healthy…a girl.'

'Then he got skeered. Maybe there's other Injuns here-abouts? He din't want nobody followin' him. So he lugged th' carcass o' th' two varmints into a big cut in th' rocks, threw 'em down there, an' dumped rocks from th' cache on top of 'em. Then he got th' five horses an' started off fer Stalnaker's, a four day ride.'

'Papaw said th' varmints done him some good, since he ended up with three extry horses, th' varmint's rifle, an English-steel tomahawk o' a kind he'd never seed before, an' a skinnin' knife better than th' one he was usin'. He warn't one bit happy with a baby, an' kept thinkin' he'd jes' throw th' damn thing over a big cliff somewhar. Who would know? But he di'n't. He give me b'ar fat dipped in cooked mash an' said I sucked on it on it like it war a milk tit. I never cried oncet.'

'When he got to Stalnaker's, he hunkered down an' waited fer an idea. Two half-breed women with a passel of youngun's commenced to giving Papaw all kinds o' advice. Finally, one o' 'em brought over a girl, a white girl, not a half-breed. I don't know how old she was, but Papaw said she war 'old enough' an' I guess I know what he meant by that. She 'lowed as she would go with him an' help with th' baby. Papaw said that warn't enough. She'd have to help with th' hides, make soap, cook up his squirrel meat. She said she would.'

'That was it.'

'She said her name was Sally Sizemore. Paw never tole me whar she come from. Sally named me Delilah, but nobody never called me by that. Jes' Lilah. An' she's th' one me an' Mason called Mamaw. She was Mason's Mamaw all right, but SHE warn't th' one that born me.'

'Well, Papaw said he was feeling right pleased. He sold two horses at Stalnaker's an' bought two iron kettles, a great big one to make salt in, an' a small one for ever' thing else, two axe heads an' a mawl, some copper for a corn still, fish hooks, an' enough seeds, needles-and-thread, an' pig iron, to fill th' bags on three horses. An' that was it. He warn't 'bout to hang around one minute longer. He didn't mind tradin' at Stalnaker's, but fer him it was too fer from Th' Woods. He wanted to stay back in Th' Wilderness. He hated laws, all laws, an' he just couldn't wait to bust out o' there. If he said it oncet, he said it a hunnerd' times, 'I jus' cain't STAND livin' all cooped up, people watchin' at you, tellin' on you…A man's not a man if he's not free to do whatever th' God Damn Hell he WANTS to do!' An' ever' time he said it, Papaw'd spit 'backer juice 'bout ten yards down th' path.'

'I war a babe an' don't 'member none of it. But Mamaw told me. They set out with three horses, me suckin' on cooked-up corn mash, or jerky soaked till it was soft. Mamaw warn't sure where they was or where they war headin', but th' trip took six days. They went up a long valley, over a little Gap, then up another valley, this one longer than th' first, then up a long creek, over a hill, then up another. Valleys, creeks, an' hollers. Finally, Paw spied a place where they was a big rock ledge stickin' out.'Hells bells! This place don't even need a roof!"

'An' that's where I growed up. Th' first year we was just closed up under th' ledge with poles, mud daubed 'roun' to keep out th' wind. Nex' year Paw chopped down some poplar trees, and hewed logs fer a cabin. Mamaw an' Mason an' me liked th' cabin. But Paw warn't hardly ever there, always out huntin'. Fact is, I don't think he had airy mind o' livin' with no Old Woman. He jes' hankered to sit out in th' woods, an' wait for some beast to come along…an' shoot hit. I think he never would-a settled down a-tall, if it hadn't been fer me, a baby.'

'At first we had jes' a dirt floor, but next year Papaw put in some puncheon logs, an' that was our floor after that. Paw chopped down more trees an' Mamaw planted corn, 'backer, Cushaw squash, shucky beans, 'taters, pumpkins, apples, peach pits. We'd go out in th' woods fer sallet greens an' diff'rent kind o' nuts; we liked black walnut th' best. But them nuts was all good, which is why squirrels and b'ars and hogs went fer 'em. Paw was still buying jug whiskey at Stalnaker's, but after a year or so, he started brewin' up mash hiss'ef. We didn't hardly need nothin'. We liked th' quiet. Nobody t' bother us, nobody messin' with us. It suited us real good. We figgered out how to make a lot o' stuff ourse'fs. If they was somethin' we couldn't make, Paw would set off with a packload o' hides, an' come back with some store-bought-cloth, or maybe thread. Oncet he come back with four pigs strapped on th' back o' his two horses. Them pigs went wild in th' woods, an' ever' year a'ter that we got good hog-meat off'n 'em. An' th' year after that, Paw come back with a spinning wheel an' some baby sheep. We didn't *need* no sheep or pigs, cause we was eatin' good off turkey, deer, an' b'ar meat, them b'ars greasy fat from th' woods bein' full o' chestnut mast. But I guess Paw figgered his Old Woman could maybe spin wool…make him somethin'.'

'Paw 'membered about blacksmith work from when he was a boy. Th' first blacksmith thing he made was some fool trapshun with a grit stone so Mamaw could grind up corn so he could brew his whisky. Later on, he kind of got into blacksmith work, and made barrel hoops, worked on his rifle, and made all kinds o' animal traps. An' that's when he started sellin' beaver pelts.'

'By this time I had growed up. I warn't sure how old I was, but I knowed I was mighty OLD, maybe seventeen. I guess I woulda been married by then…'cept we was back so fer up th' holler, nobody ever' come 'roun'.'

Then Simon Begley come along. He an' Papaw got along all right cause Simon was A Hunter just like him…An' neither one of 'em ever farmed a lick.'

'Well, that got Papaw started thinking'. He an' Simon were pullin' at th' jug purty hard. They went on 'bout how awful OLD I was. But, *maybe*, I might be young enough to git married. Papaw an' Simon finally agreed that was a right smart idea.'

'So I went off with him. Paw told Simon that he guessed if he was gonna keep an Old Woman, he'd have to build a cabin, an' Simon 'lowed as how he might do that. But Paw warned him good. He dad-blamed did NOT want no neighbors. NOBODY! Simon had to move at least three ridges, maybe FIVE ridges, away. Paw said 'I just cain't STAND people crowdin' up.'

'So that's what Simon did. He built us a little cabin a day's ride away. An' little Maggie…yore Mama…was born ten months later.'

'So I recken that makes you part Injun, jes' like me. I never saw my Cherokee mama. But I guess you might have maybe one part Injun blood, five parts white man's blood.' Lilah looked into the distance. 'I'm half-Injun, an' I look it, an' it don't bother me none. I never could deposit what people have agin' Injuns. They'd leave us be if w'd leave them be. They taught us a lot 'bout how to live in th' woods.'

'An' Paw…' Lilah's voice trailed off, and she suddenly seemed OLDER. 'Well, by this time, I'd been with Simon a good spell, 'cause yore Mama was near full growed. Mamaw tole me Paw had gone out huntin'. Just like he always done. He'd been gone maybe two weeks, when one morning both his horses come up to Mamaw's cabin. They knowed th' way back. Th' lead horse had Paw's rifle in its saddle case. Th' second, tied to it, was loaded with hides. But Paw warn't with 'em.'

'Mamaw sent Mason out huntin' fer 'im, but Mason had nairy a notion o' where to look, so he come back. Then she sent over fer Simon an' me. It took Mason two days to *find* Simon. Then th' three o' us…Mason, Simon, an' me…went out lookin' fer Paw. We hunted fer days. Simon could track *good*. But he couldn't find airy a trace ANY-WHERES. So we come back.'

'There warn't hardly nobody ever' come through way back at th' head o' th' holler where we was. But we ast everbody that did come through. An' Simon ast ever' time he went to trade his hides. Nairy a soul knew a thang! Paw jes' disappeared! We didn't bury him...nor nothin'....' Her voice trailed off softly.

'I have pondered till my head hurt an' still don't have airy idea. No idea a-tall. Was he kilt by Injuns? Maybe a rock fell off a cliff an' hit him in the haid? Maybe he got a fever an' fell off his horse an' couldn't get back on? I wisht I *knew*.'

'But that war the end o' Paw. *That war the end o' Ward Gilley.* He jes' *vanished*...in seventeen an' ninety-one.'

She took a long puff on her pipe and looked into space. 'I want ye to have Paw's rifle. Hit's th' onliest thing lef' that war truly his'n...Keep hit SAFE, now!'

James Broughton often went hunting with his father-in-law. Simon Begley never once tried to grow anything. No farming for him; he was A Hunter, and made his living off hides and pelts. He often said, '*Game is so thick, you cain't NEVER hunt it out.* Deer in all seasons, an' squirrel meat fer ever' meal. Big flocks o' pigeons; so thick, you jes' hit 'em with a stick. We fed th' squabs to th' hogs.' But as the years wore on, Begley had to trek farther and farther for elk, be out weeks at a time. And there were no buffalo or wolves...ANYWHERE. 'N'airy a one. You kin find a few b'ar or gobblers, but even they seem more skase ever' season.'

By 1823, when his brother Robert built The Mill, only a few were alive who had ever heard the hideous HOWLS in the night. As the elders talked, stark terror would sweep over them. Some trembled. One old man, his voice quavering, said: 'Hit was strange! Spooky! Like a ha'nt! If ye heerd it oncet, ye'd never fergit it. Like th' howl o' a Ghost, or a Dead Man, or *Th' Devil hisse'f*! That beast was jes' HOWLIN' at th' moon! That there howl is...TH' MOUNTAIN PAINTER!'

After Robert started grinding meal and sawing logs, James said 'he never agin' met a single soul who had hisSE'F had ever heerd a painter.'

'Maybe they was all shot out?'

* * * * *

[See *Sons of a Trackless Forest: The Cumberland Long Hunters of the Eighteenth Century*, Mark A. Baker, 1999, Baker's Trace Publishing, Franklin, Tennessee.]

THE SETTLER
HARGIS BROUGHTON 1759–1823

◆

The boy's main job was hunting game for food…for The Surveyor, for himself, and for Ezra the camp boy, a slave loaned by Colonel Patton. Every few days Hargis left at dawn for the woods. He was getting much better with the long rifle, but he still wasted powder and shot. Nonetheless he always brought back, usually well before sundown, sometimes a deer haunch, sometimes a turkey, or, if nothing else, a pouch of rabbits or squirrels, which were killed without a wound if the ball hit the bark by their heads. He and Ezra would gut, clean, carve, and cook the meat. They also salted some so he didn't have to hunt every day. Meals also included hoecake, hominy, parched corn, and meal, bought at a Factor's Depot in Wolf Hills.

Broughton and Ezra also pitched the tents, a big one for The Surveyor, and a little one he and Ezra shared. The two sometimes talked at night. Ezra said he had been born on Colonel Patton's Plantation, 'jus' like my Mammy an' Pappy. My Gran'mammy's Maw was from some other Plantation, don' know whar. She run away an' took up with th' Cherokee in th' woods. A'ter 'bout six months, Settlers snuk up on 'em, an' ever' Injun man was kilt. She run away agin, but th' Settlers caught her. Well, when they brung her back to her Plantation, her Owner said he warn't 'bout to keep no Slave that run away. So he took her down to Williamsburg an' sold her to Colonel Patton. 'Bout three months later she had a baby, half-Injun. That baby was my Gran'mammy.'

Broughton and Ezra loaded tents, bedding, and surveying gear on the packhorse and the mule, a full load for two animals. The Surveyor rode a fine buckskin stallion. In morning light or at sunset, its coat, which The Surveyor insisted Ezra brush twice a day, shone like burnished gold. Hargis and Ezra walked behind the two pack animals. They didn't travel far because The Surveyor had to stop every so often…to peer at his watch, squint at the sun through his sextant, select distinctive features as landmarks, make calculations, and write everything in his leather bound book. Broughton could not read or write. He understood very little of what The Surveyor did, or why, and not a single iota of the geometry. But he watched, and he slowly acquired a vague notion. One thing he was quite sure of: there was no chance at all that the outcome of The Survey would be favorable to an ordinary person like him.

Broughton's main task, aside from supplying food, was to work with Ezra to move the chain, and the chaining-pins and flags. They did their best to follow The Surveyor's instructions, but they often could not hear him. This obliged them to run back to make sure they knew what he wanted them to do. Sometimes they understood his arm signals…left up, right up, both out…

The Surveyor specified that Broughton, and absolutely NOT Ezra, carry and fix the chaining-pins and flags, the Gunter's chain…twenty-two yards long, one hundred links, and The Jacob's Staff, which supported the compass. And he absolutely forbade EITHER of them to so much as TOUCH the precious theodolite or compass. He and he alone removed them from their padded cases, carefully mounted them, squinted through them, and then, handling them with great delicacy, stowed them back in their cases. When Broughton and Ezra had moved the chains and flags the way The Surveyor wanted, and after he had peered through his telescope and compass, he would go off by himself, like it was a secret or something, and work with his maps and drafting tools. That was when Broughton and Ezra could take a little rest.

Colonel James Patton, who was mapping a new section of southwest Virginia for The Wood River Land Company, employed them all. Broughton had a very low opinion of Land Companies. To him, they were just one more way for The Gentry and mucky-mucks to steal and lord it over The Poor Man. He wished to God! He knew some way he could get IN on the scheme! Owning land meant big houses, Plantations, and lots of slaves to do the work. There was NO WAY an ordinary mortal could gain access to this enterprise. The Families had it locked up. It was A Closed Corporation…no outsiders, no riffraff, allowed.

So far as he could tell, The Families were all Related one way or another, or did Business together, or went to the same Church, or Voted Together in The Council. In Williamsburg, The Families voted each other enormous grants of land in the unknown Western backwoods of Virginia, The Wilderness that lay just over The Blue Ridge…800,000 acres to The Loyal Land Company, a nearly equal amount to The Ohio Company, vast acreage to The Greenbrier Company. Of course the Land Companies made sure The Governor and The King received proper quitrents. They distributed handbills extolling the supposed fertility of the new lands, hoping to lure Settlers, who were allowed to pay over time. Granting backwoods land enriched both Colony and Mother Country…more people, more money from export of tobacco, therefore more money to buy manufactured goods from England…which made The Board of Trade in London happy. Some land grants required Treaties with Indians, which often required tedious palaver. But Treaties were do-able, quite do-able. The Indians were all dying of The Pox anyway.

Broughton did not at first realize the important role of Surveyors in this scheme. But over the months it slowly came to him: Surveyors were often the first Europeans into new frontier areas. They could therefore spot and patent the most valuable land for themselves and their friends. A reliable Surveyor was indispensable if your object was to grab as much Western land as you could. And the Pursuit of Land was the chief aim of all influential Virginians.

Broughton was not sure how his mother and father, and theirs before them, had ended up in Northern Ireland. He only knew they had been driven out of Scotland and, as Presbyterians, were hated equally by Irish Catholics AND by The Church of England. At age ten he began work as slop boy for a Belfast butcher. The work was so long and hard, and his prospects so grim, he did not see how he could possibly do worse than Take a Chance on The New World. At fifteen, he paid for his passage by agreeing to four years' labor.

He was Indented by an Agent who represented six Virginia Planters. They wanted carpenters, bricklayers, and mechanics…but were obliged to settle for what they could get, usually raw labor, no skills at all. The Agent also worked free-lance, and side-deals with ship's Captains were profitable for both. The Agent was trying, in the three days before sailing, to assemble enough human cargo to negotiate a reduced fare per head. He would of course pocket the savings. Time was running short and The Agent thought he might have to fill the Manifest with Involuntary Indentures…felons, ragamuffins, debtors, military prisoners, dissenters…any dregs or rejects The Crown would be pleased to cast out. Either way, Agents and Captains profited nicely.

Hargis thought it was 'the year 17 and 75' when they docked in Philadelphia. He thought that date was on his Indent, but he was unable to read it, had it been shown to him, which it was not. His foot had been on land no more than an hour before a two-mule wagon pulled up to fetch him and six others. They rattled down The Great Wagon Road, a broad natural boulevard of beauty and history, the most heavily traveled highway in all America. There were ferries and fords, and inns and taverns every few miles, people heading north, heading south, Indian traders, missionaries, frontier militias, itinerant peddlers. Most were families heading West, seeking land they could settle and own…improve with their labor…and create a better future.

The wagon passed through Lancaster, York, Gettysburg, Harper's Ferry. Hargis and two others were dumped off at Staunton Court House and warned, 'Don't move one single foot from this spot.' The driver said The Road continued to Lexington; at Big Lick, it forked to Kings Mountain, Cowpens, Guilford Courthouse, Winston-Salem, Salisbury, Charlotte, The Yadkin Valley, and Watauga. Another route linked Wolf Hills to The Wilderness Road in Southwestern Virginia. A new extension of The Road was opening via the Holston, Clinch and Powell valleys to Gaps in the Cumberland and Pine mountains, and via Boone's Trace or Scagg's Trace to Kaintuck.

Another wagon soon arrived to take them to a Plantation on The James, half in Albemarle, half in Fluvanna County. Hargis had never been a farmer and knew nothing about farming, with the possible exception of how to bludgeon an ox and carve out its guts. But that didn't matter. The Plantation needed men and there were not enough workers, slave or free. The Overseer put him in the fields the day he arrived, chopping weeds, hoeing corn, suckering tobacco. He crowded in with three others in a tiny cabin far back of The Big House. Field hands, indented or slave, were given any Big House food that was uneaten and likely to spoil. But their main diet was meal, hominy, chitlin's and hog fat, and greens such as cushaw blossoms, wild poke-weed, plantain, and speckled jack. He had to beg for clothing. The work was hard, but he had worked harder lugging butcher's slop. He could take it.

The Plantation encouraged field hands to attend church, one for Whites, one for Slaves. Despite his low opinion of religion generally, Hargis went a few times his first year. The Preacher, The Overseer's cousin, had only one sermon, 'Sin and The Eternal Fires of Hell,' a straightforward message repeated with almost no variation: Sin is universal; every person, even a baby, is A Sinner, even though one might be totally unaware of this Fact; only a few Chosen or Elect, known but to God, will be spared the Fires of Hell. Since Hargis viewed his labor on the Plantation as very close to Damnation right here on Earth, he concluded he did not require further Instruction on this point. His antipathy toward religion was confirmed, and he never went again.

He counted the years, and when his time was up, 'in 17 and 79,' he had acquired a little familiarity with farming, or at least the hot sun labor of it, though the tobacco-and-slave barons of Virginia practiced the most wasteful kind of agronomy, preferring to mine topsoil for a few years, then begin a new Plantation on virgin land, usually toward the West.

Hargis asked all the others, white and black, what he ought to do. Few ventured an opinion; most confessed they didn't rightly know. Some thought it might be exciting to 'jine up' with a militia. 'They is War ever' whar. Th' Families think they don't need no King no more. Some say The Planters will run Virginia they se'ves.' Others had heard stories about good land in Kaintuck, free for the taking, though they weren't quite sure where Kaintuck was or how to get there. In fact, there were so many stories about the place, a few of them possibly true, ministers started warning congregations against 'The Buzzel.' There were also stories of Indian capture and hideous torture. Indian terror was the most common subject of gossip everywhere, even in The Big House.

Hargis didn't have much use for the Overseer, who treated everyone equally, with raw contempt. But his opinion of the man improved a bit the day he let him go, as he generously allowed Hargis to keep the clothes he had on his back, the ones he had worked and slept in, a heavily patched shirt of osnaburg linen, leather breeches, and a coat of canvas and blanket wool. He even let him keep an old felt hat with a hole in it, and a butcher knife with no handle. Indian Terror or not…Hargis set out walking, heading southwest.

The prospect of good land, free for the taking, was simply irresistible. He had one shilling, sixpence in his pocket, earned from selling possum skins. He slept in fields and stole any food he could. It took him ten days to reach Wolf Hills. He didn't know if that was where his luck changed for the Better, or where it changed for the Worse. *But his luck certainly Changed.*

The Trading Post at Wolf Hills was rough, as was everything this far West. But the man buying goods was not at all rough…and was therefore completely out of place. Hargis thought he must be A Gentleman, to judge by his fine clothing, not a patch on it, his smooth way of talking, and the fact that he had a slave manservant with him. Hargis tried to make conversation. Indian terror stories seemed like a good way to start.

The Surveyor was curt. 'Don't believe everything you hear.'

Hargis said, 'I don't.'

He looked The Gentleman over sideways, so he wouldn't notice. His boots were caked with mud. And the goods he was buying could only mean he was heading into The Woods. But *which* Woods? *Where* was he heading?

'I've served out my Contrack. I'm looking fer work.'

'Let me see your Paper.' Hargis produced what the Overseer had given him, awkwardly tugging his forelock like his ancestors before him.

'If…I say *if*…I take you on, you must do *every single thing* I tell you, *exactly* the way I tell you to do it, and you must do it *quick*. No back talk. I don't have time for sass. I pay one pound a month.'

Hargis just stared. He had no idea at all what The Surveyor meant.

'Well? Are you deaf? What do you say?'

Hargis mumbled something, and the deed was done. The Surveyor said, 'Ezra will show you what to do. Go help him load the horse and mule.'

He stayed with The Surveyor ten months, traveling over a wide area of southwest Virginia. He learned the names of the trees and plants, and over time became an excellent hunter. He also picked up as much woodcraft as The Surveyor deigned to show him. He even used a strip of deerskin to tie his hair in a pigtail, just like The Surveyor did. When they got as far West as the trading post on The Long Island of The Holston, he asked for his ten pounds, and quit. Hargis had no idea what he would do, or where he would go.

The Surveyor planned to stay a few days at Long Island. He had to write and post some letters, he needed supplies, and he needed to hire a new flag boy. Most importantly of all, he had to call on Settlers that had squatted on Colonel Patton's land nearby. His employer was the fairest man in all Virginia. All he asked was that the squatters make their Mark on A Paper, which none could read, acknowledging that they had cleared and occupied land, per Plat of Metes and Bounds, that belonged to The Colonel, and that this Paper was their legal Promise to Pay. In the matter of payment, The Surveyor regarded The Colonel as a veritable paragon of generosity. He gave the squatters ten years to pay, one-tenth per year. If they were unable to pay in cash, he would graciously accept their hogs or cattle or horses. What could be more Generous, more Fair, than that? But of course if they did Not Pay, he would bring Law Men with Guns, and force them off.

A family was at The Trading Post, buying supplies. They said they intended to follow Boone's Trace into Kaintuck, but allowed as how they might have to wait a spell for others. Families had to travel together, as it was 'MADNESS to travel alone.' That meant 'CERTAIN capture by Indians, and DEATH BY TORTURE.'

The head of the family said his name was Frazer Tolbert. He was a slight, wiry man, perhaps forty years of age, a bundle of taut energy. He had farmed a little, 'mostly corn and 'backer, but huntin's what I like best.' He was born in Pennsylvania and had hunted all over that Colony. He and his family had just come up from Carolina because game was starting to get shot out. 'It was plum downright sca'se in Watauga. Your fambly'll never go hungry if'n you know how to hunt good. But 'course ye got to have th' game. We heered 'bout easy game EVERwheres in

Kaintuck. An' land free fer th' takin'. So that's where we're goin'. We might leave tomorrer if'n another bunch shows up.'

Tolbert had six children, and his wife was heavily pregnant. His four boys looked sullen and mean, his two older girls looked sullen and stupid. If one kept an Account, Tolbert's 'fambly' would be entered as a Debit, in fact, a Total Loss. On the Asset side, Tolbert possessed two Pennsylvania rifles, three axes, and six iron kettles, three of them cracked. His little caravan was led by a sound bay mare, tied in tandem to three other heavily laden pack horses, these latter so beat-up and splayed it was not clear they would survive the trip. Tolbert said, "Spect I'll need ALL my goods over in Kaintuck.'

Hargis and Tolbert talked at length about 'Injuns.' The only ones Hargis had seen were three Cherokee men, and their women and children, on their way to trade at Great Lick. But he had heard stories. LOTS of stories.

Tolbert began. 'I say they're Devils. They don't come at you face-on like white men, but hide back in th' forest. Ye never SEE 'em, never HEAR 'em. They leap out fast as lightnin'. It don't matter none to them if it's a growed man, or a woman, or a baby. All th' same. They scalp ever' one. Then they kill all th' wounded so they can git away quick. An' they WANT to hurt you as bad as they can. They LIKE it if'n they can make you scream. If they grab you, I say, Pray to God! Pray to God fer a quick death! That's th' only way out. But us Hunters is tough. We know how to fight. We WILL fight back…And *we aim to win*. I'm a Christian man…but *I'd be doin' God's work to kill any Injun I could.*'

Then it was Hargis' turn: He repeated a story he heard from a field hand on the Plantation. 'They was a flatboat floating down th' Ohio, but ever' person on it was dead. They found an Injun's fingers chopped off where he had tried to climb in. You hear all kind of stories. I hear tell that some that went to Kaintuck is clearing out cause th' Shawnee is killin' 'em all. Women-folk, an' th' men too, is all crazy with fear. None of 'em cain't take it no more.'

Tolbert could top this, easy. 'Well, them little pole stockades they built up thar in Kaintuck don't slow down th' Shawnee one bit. Settlers crowded in like pigs, no winders, no air. Shawnees got so bold they had to send th' men out in twos, one bunch to plant, th' other bunch to patrol aroun' so they warn't scalped. An' if they do get a crop planted, th' Injuns come back an' poison it. An' they steal. They sneak in an' steal ever' little thing. They steal horses an' rifles th' most. I heered two hunnerd horses was stole in Kaintuck jes' this year.'

Hargis thought his story was better. 'Well, I heerd that th' Injuns burned one man's boy right in front of his eyes. An' there was a woman in a cabin, th' Injuns busted in, kilt her husband an' all her youngun's. She slept that night on th' cabin floor in th' middle o' their blood. An' I heered 'bout one man an' his wife. Th' Injuns caught 'em, tore off their clothes an' tied 'em to saplings. They cut into their bellies, pulled out a piece o' their guts, an' tied that piece to th' sapling. Then they forced 'em to walk roun' an' roun' th' sapling…till their guts was all pulled out.'

Tolbert said, 'An' those they don't kill, they carry off an' sell. Or adopt 'em, turn 'em into Injuns, an' they don't know their own white people no more.'

Hargis asked a reasonable question, 'But if it's so bad, and we are shore as sartin' to be kilt, why would we aim to go thar?'

Tolbert's response was so compelling Hargis realized it was pointless to respond: *"Cause we are God-fearin' people*! God KNOWS! An' He will protect us! Th' Injuns ain't GOT no God. It's them that does th' Devil's work. I ain't 'shamed to say I'm skeered o' th' Devil, an' skeered o' Injuns. But God tole Adam to 'fill the earth an' subdue it'. That's what Th' Bible says. An' I aim to do it. Anyways, Injuns ain't like white men. They is savages…an' heathens. They got hardly no goods at all, which PROVES how lazy an' stupid they is. They trek all over th' land, but all they do is hunt. That's a plumb waste o' good farm land! God don't want land to lay fallow. A Christian has a RIGHT to settle that land. God GIVE us that land! God TOLE us to make it multiply. We can build ourse'fs a cabin, grow a crop, raise our fambly. It was GOD! who give us that right. Kaintuck's the new Promised Land!'

Tolbert knew this was The Topper, and that he had won the Debate. He puffed up…and unlimbered a Barlow knife to cut himself a big boot of chaw from a twist of tobacco.

The Surveyor had listened to this exchange, but had not interrupted. 'You may be right. Or not. I don't say I am an expert on Indians…Shawnee, Cherokee, Wyandot, any of them. But I think they are pretty much like us, at least in some ways. Some of them are good, some are bad. I've known a few good ones. I think they mainly just want to be left alone. Fact is, and you know it, we're pushing them hard, pushing them West, pushing them out of their hunting lands. If you think on it, you can see how you might get riled up too.' And with that, The Surveyor paid The Trader, turned sharply, and went out the door. He leashed his packhorse and mule to his handsome stallion, and, with Ezra the slave boy trudging behind, rode back toward the east.

Coming to The New World was a Gamble, but Hargis was beginning to think he had Lost the Bet. In fact, he was pretty sure he had Lost. He Indented himself for four years' labor, hoping he might learn a trade or, somehow, anyhow, better his condition. Everybody called Virginia 'a glorious country, a Land of Opportunity.' Everybody said, 'It's A New World, somethin' better, somethin' diff'rent. A young man willing to work can make A Fortune.'

But this had not happened. Hargis had sweated till he thought he would drop, working hard, very hard. Four years a field hand, and what did he have to show? NOT ONE THING! His Best Chance had been with The Surveyor. He had Ten Pounds in his pocket. But he had Lost the Bet yet again. He thought to himself, 'I was A FOOL! to let The Surveyor walk out The Post!'

Day followed day, but still no 'famblys' heading toward Kaintuck.

A few showed up to trade: three Settlers who said their farms were 'a day down th' path'…a Hunter buying powder and lead, and six half-breeds…whose skin color and features suggested an amazing admixture of white, Indian and African…trading pelts for English steel tomahawks and knives.

Hargis began to exchange a few words with the two Tolbert girls, Hannah who said she was "bout fourteen,' and Mayme, who looked perhaps seventeen. With more acquaintance, he began to alter his opinion. Maybe the girls were a tad less sullen, a bit less stupid, than he thought. Mayme was the smarter and prettier of the two, with the freckled ivory skin and red hair of many Scots and Irish. Hargis and Mayme started talking quietly. Once, they went off alone in the woods when her parents were busy cooking.

Tolbert and his family camped and waited. He and Hargis talked for two weeks, half the time imagining the PARADISE in Kaintuck, half the time imagining unspeakable TERROR in Kaintuck.

Tolbert's every utterance was punctuated with allusions to God and visions of boundless prospects. 'A fine strong young man like you could make it GOOD in Kaintuck. I'll be durd if'n I wouldn't do it, young as you is. There's rich land all over, cane so thick on it you KNOW it'll make a fine crop. Plenty o' game ever' whar. If we stick together, th' Injuns won't dare come at us.'

Then Sturgill arrived. He was short and thick, all muscle, no fat, his face burnt red by long days of clearing fields and plowing. He rode a small mule, leading a bigger mule and two horses, loaded down with what seemed to be every pot and pan he owned. His wife and two girls, faces shielded by bonnets, all barefoot, lurked behind, but managed to keep up. Ambrose, his older boy, ran ahead.

Sturgill said he 'busted out' trying to farm 'backer in Carolina. 'I aim to make a new farm over in Kaintuck…If'n I kin find th' right Road. I figgered they might be somun here-abouts could point out Th' Kentucky Road.'

Tolbert grew agitated with excitement. 'We are might proud you-uns showed up! Kin you jine up with us? Name's Tolbert…what's your'n?'

'Sturgill.'

'Is that yer given name?'

'Hit's Virgil. But nobody don't call me by that. Just Sturgill.' He turned to The Trader, hopeful, quizzical. 'We're aimin' to foller Th' Kentucky Road. Do you know how to git to it?' The Trader said nothing.

Tolbert jumped right in. 'Why Hell's Bells, Man! There ain't nairy a thing to it! Th' Road is as plain as anything. Judge Henderson sent out axemen, an' that Road is blazed clear all th' way to Fort Boone. Five hundred souls has followed that Trace already. I been waitin' here fer another fambly, so we kin go together. Hit's safer like that.'

Sturgill and Tolbert talked the rest of the day. Each owned a few head of cattle and some hogs which they had left behind in Watauga, planning to send back for them 'after we get settled.' They then unloaded their pack animals, and inventoried every bit of gear they carried. They calculated they needed two more bags of meal apiece, and more powder and shot.

Then both of them started in on Hargis.

'Now boy, you ain't got a horse, and you ain't got no rifle, no axe, no pots, no nothin'! How in THE WORLD do you 'spect to git to Kaintuck an' make a crop if you ain't fitted out right? If you aim to git to Kaintuck, jine up with us. Th' Trader says a farmer here-abouts has a horse fer sale. I got an extry rifle, an' we may NEED that gun if'n we run into trouble. Kin ye shoot?'

The next two days were spent dickering with the farmer about his horse, testing Hargis to make sure he knew how to handle a rifle, and haggling with The Trader about prices: a tomahawk, knife, meal, powder and shot, and supplies Tolbert said Hargis HAD to have. By the time Tolbert was satisfied that Hargis was 'fitted out,' his Ten Pounds were entirely gone. Hargis would set out for Kaintuck without a cent...*in debt* to Tolbert for an axe and a rifle.

On The Sabbath, Tolbert led the group in prayers, followed by a long harangue, punctuated by banging on a Bible. 'Kaintuck is The New

Eden, an' we will settle it jes' like th' first Man an' th' first Woman in Th'
Garden. *God is watching over us an' He will see us through!* Amen! Say
'Amen!' somebody!' They spent The Sabbath afternoon loading their
animals for The Journey.

Just after dawn on a Monday in April 1779, the party set out, heading
North toward The Wilderness Road. All walked…Tolbert first, leading
four pack horses, his wife and six children straggling behind. Sturgill
was next, leading four pack animals, two horses and two mules, his wife
and three children walking alongside. Hargis led his new horse, loaded
with provisions Tolbert insisted he bring. Fortunately, the mare was big
and strong, the farmer having used it mainly for pulling stumps.

Tolbert had enquired earnestly of every person that might have any
inkling. By the time they left Long Island, he was overflowing with
enthusiasm and confidence: 'Ain't NO WAY we can git lost! The Road
starts right HERE!'

They headed north toward The Block House established by Colonel
John Anderson, which they reached the next day. They found good
grass for their animals, and a pleasant clearing in which to camp.
Hargis, on the basis of his experience with The Surveyor, was chosen
chief Hunter, and returned after a few hours with a buck deer. The
Colonel was not at The Block House, having been called back to Fort
Chiswell, but ragged militiamen showed them the faint trace of a foot-
path, which they said was The Kentucky Road.

Tolbert was eager, and they set off early the next day, following a
rough trail through Moccasin Gap, which they had traversed by sundown. Tolbert was, as always, full of energy and encouragement, especially when they came within sight or hailing distance of others heading
West. And, more good luck, The Trace was now better marked. The next
destination was Glade Spring.

'Praise God! We'uns are plumb in th' middle of th' Valley of Th'
Powell river. From here on to Martin's Station is all flat ground. We got
to keep a sharp eye for Injuns, but as fer as Th' Trace, why we kin' jes'

saunter down to Glade Spring. Oh! *God has blessed us!* We are bound fer Kaintuck, an' we WILL git thar, Praise Be to God!'

The Trace followed creek-beds, a watery thread winding through a wild tapestry of trees. Untold generations of fallen giants had enriched the soil with their decay, and deep black humus carpeted the forest floor from creek banks almost to the tops of the spurs. There were scattered clearings where trees had fallen from age, lightning, or high winds. This immense primeval forest, so dense as to be very nearly a jungle, was choked with centuries-old tangles of rhododendron, wild grapevines and thickets of holly. Walnut, white and red oak, chestnut, hickory, beech, cucumber magnolia, black gum, persimmon, and many other species grew in the wildest profusion on hillside, cove, and valley floor. The giants of the forest were the yellow poplars, some ten feet in diameter, straight as arrows and centuries old, so tall their tops could not be seen. Foliage was so dense little sunlight reached the forest floor, and the hollows and valleys were dark and menacing. In the branches of these great trees, thriving on mast, were armies of squirrels, the foremost delicacy of frontier cuisine. It was April and dogwood and redbud provided splashes of color amid the trees, while jack-in-the-pulpit were swelling into bloom. The woods were full of birds...wood thrush singing in nests, yellow-headed Carolina parrots feeding in cocklebur patches, woodpeckers hammering noisily in tall snag trees, owls flapping silently in the night. Creek banks were often choked with cane, tall plants which formed a thick wall, shutting out all light.

Axemen had blazed A Trace...but it was still VERY tough going. Heading West from Martin's Station, the soaring limestone escarpment of Cumberland Mountain began to loom on their right, and they soon spied the famous White Cliffs. 'We're close! Mighty close!,' Tolbert cried. Just then his wife sent Hannah running forward to tell him to stop. *RIGHT NOW!* 'Maw says her waters has busted, an' she thinks th' baby's comin.'

Tolbert was not a bit happy about stopping, especially since they were no more than a day from The Gap and Kaintuck. He was torn between his eagerness to reach what he was beginning to think of as The Promised Land, and his tender feelings toward his wife. The confusion showed on his face.

But he had no choice. The party stopped, unloaded their baggage and made camp. A canvas tent was erected for his wife, and Sturgill's wife took turns with Tolbert, tending his wife as she moaned in labor. She lay crying with pain, sometimes screaming out, for two full days and nights.

But no baby.

Sturgill's wife suggested lifting her onto her feet, or moving her into various positions. But she was no midwife, and had no idea of what to do. They tried everything they could think of, even massaging her belly.

Still, no baby.

Tolbert began to be worried, and said so: 'The other young'uns all come easy.' All he could do was pray, which he did: 'God, you brung us this fer, an' we trust You will keep us safe. Please God, show yer Mercy on my wife an' th' young'un that's tryin' to be born! Amen! *SAY AMEN! somebody.*'

The baby made its appearance on the third day, a girl. Tolbert's wife was bleeding heavily, and it never stopped. She made a great effort, but was too weak to hold the baby to her breast. Sturgill's wife cooked soft food that might keep the baby alive. Tolbert's wife remained in the tent, moaning softly…a fifth day, a sixth day. By now she had a high fever, her body soaked with sweat, her skin cold and clammy to the touch. She was unable to keep food down. She was deathly pale, and too weak to raise her head.

Tolbert said he would stay by his wife's side, but asked Sturgill to ride back to Martin's Station to see if there was 'a Granny Woman' or 'ANY soul who knows how to help with birthin'.'

Sturgill returned the next morning with an old woman carrying a sack of herbs and tonics, which, judging by effect, seemed to be powerful emetics and purgatives. Tolbert's wife grew worse. She was delirious, and her weak cries made no sense. The party had now camped for nine days.

All that Tolbert could do was communicate with God. He went off alone into the woods, but his voice carried. 'God! Lord God Almighty! We aim to do Thy Will. We trust in you, Lord! *You have The Power!* You kin save this woman! We just cain't make it in Kaintuck without her! An' the youngun's? How will THEY make it?! Thy Will be done! Thy Will Be Done, Lord! But save her! *Almighty God, we beg You to Save This Woman!'*

Tolbert's wife died late the next evening.

There was little to say, but there was work to do. The next morning, Tolbert, Sturgill and Hargis selected a chestnut nearby and chopped it down, working hard to hew it with mawls and wedges. The labor seemed to comfort Tolbert, who attacked the log as though he were smiting Evil itself. The result was crude, more hollow log than coffin, but it was all they had. Then Tolbert called a halt. 'We all need a rest. We've had all we kin take fer now.'

He went alone into the woods.

They buried her the next afternoon. That morning, her two daughters cleared away the bloody rags and washed their mother's clothing, biting their lips to keep from crying. They dried her clothes in the sun, then put them back on her body. They arranged her hair, and came back from the woods with mountain ivy. It was not yet in bloom, but buds were beginning to show a blush of pink and white. It was the prettiest plant they could find.

Hargis and Sturgill dug the grave. Tolbert looked defeated, slumped in despair, his speech interrupted by heavy gasps. Tolbert asked Sturgill to 'say some words.' Hargis and Sturgill lifted the coffin into the grave. Then Sturgill said, 'I'm not good at talkin', an' I'm not much fer church-goin', an' I jes' don't know what to say. This here was a Good Woman, an' her husbin' is a God-fearin' man. We are mighty sorry fer her an' her husbin' an' their youngun's. We here below don't understand God's ways. We do th' best we know how. We ast you, Lord, to look a'ter this woman up in Heaven. Let us do God's Will so we kin all meet agin by Th' Throne. We will all be united in Heaven. AMEN!'

They covered the grave with dirt, and Hargis erected the cross he had made, 'Esther Tolbert, 1743-1779.' They stood awkwardly around the grave, not knowing when, or if, to move away. Hargis mumbled a few words, trying to comfort Tolbert, who looked grim, haggard…and twenty years older.

Tolbert stared blankly at the soil covering the coffin, tears rolling down his face. He caressed his Bible tenderly, shifting it from hand to hand. Then he touched it to his face. 'I never tole this to nobody, an' I'm 'shamed to admit it now. Fact is, I cain't read. Cain't read a lick. This here Book is *Th' Word o' God*, an' I cain't read hit! Mebbe that's why God is mad at us! Do you think that's why He took Esther? We need to learn our letters, learn us how to read *Th' Word o' God!*'

Tolbert turned to his two daughters. 'Mayme, you an' Hannah is gonna hafta be Th' Mama now. Maw is gone an' we ain't got nobody else. But we WILL make it in Kaintuck! We don't KNOW God's Plan! But He WANTS us to make that land grow, make it multiply, build ourse'fs a cabin, make a crop. Maw didn't make it to Kaintuck…God's Will Be Done! AMEN!…but *WE WILL!*'

Sturgill's wife cooked meal, strained it through a cloth, and added a little meat drippings. She had no bottle or nipple, but dipped a corner of a linen cloth into the mixture, and used her finger to push it into the baby's mouth. By this time, the baby, which Tolbert named Esther in memory of his wife, was too weak to cry. Sturgill's wife said the baby had 'colick an' fever.'

The next day they began the hard climb up to The Gap. It began to rain halfway, and soon a spring storm had soaked them to the skin.

Rivulets of muddy water washed back down the mountain. The Trace wound around boulders, or edged dangerously toward precipitous cliffs. Some sections of the Trace were so steep they had to get behind the animals and push. The caravan rested a bit at The Cave, and watered the horses and mules.

The descent would have been dangerous at any time, but rain had turned The Trace into a mud hole, every step uncertain and treacherous. Animals and people slipped, stumbled, and fell. People hung on by grabbing saplings. Two horses lost their footing, went down, and could not get back up. They were unpacked completely, lifted back onto their feet, then reloaded.

When they finally reached the flat ground at Yellow Creek, they found good pasture for the animals, but no dry ground anywhere on which to camp. Tolbert and Sturgill conferred, agreeing all had been through so much, they needed some rest. Tolbert got down on one knee. 'Almighty God has Blessed us by allowing us to git this fur. We are in Kaintuck, Praise be to God! Amen.'

They had planned to set out early the next day, but Sturgill's wife said 'This young'un's got colick real bad. It cain't take much more.' They waited another day while she did everything she could to get food down the infant. By the next morning the baby was too weak to suck at all.

The baby died a few hours after nightfall. This death was different. They did not bother with a coffin, but after dawn wrapped the baby in linen and buried it immediately. Hargis fashioned a tiny cross. Tolbert said a brief prayer, his voice doleful, soft, strangled. 'I am Resigned. I am Resigned to th' Will o' Almighty God.' Sturgill and Hargis wondered if he would 'bear up.'

Early next morning, after he had prayed by himself, Tolbert packed his animals and urged them to set out. He had met another would-be Settler camped nearby whose horse had fallen over a steep cliff in The Gap. 'Broke both forelegs. Warn't nothin' to do but shoot it.' The Settler looked as though he had lost his best friend, which he had. 'Had that horse more'n ten year…A GOOD horse!' He had improvised a lean-to. 'I'm jist a-sittin' here a-waitin' fer my son to come back from Martin's Station with a horse, mule, ox, jackass or any fool beast that kin carry our goods.' He told Tolbert, 'I hear they is good grass at Wasioto. You kin make it in a day if ye start early. Ye go over Log Mountain.' They reached Wasioto as night was falling, and made a rough camp on muddy ground near a Creek that ran into the river. Sturgill said the river was The Cumberland.

The loss of his wife and infant daughter had made a great change in Tolbert. His movements were slow, his speech quavery and deliberate, his face etched with despair. He seemed to be laboring under a great weight, his back stooped, as though it was he, and not his animals, that bore his heavy gear. 'Hit's hard. Hit is mighty hard. We will git there, Lord, with Yore help. But hit is HARD! An' we ast You to he'p us, he'p us see it through.'

Sturgill and Hargis said they were worried about Tolbert, but agreed that the journey might 'ease his spirits.' Sturgill said Tolbert had asked him to 'take over.' Sturgill said, 'Right now, I think he's makin' it on spit an' grit.'

Hargis hesitated, then at last spoke what had long been on his mind. 'I know he wants to do right, an' I know he's a good, God-fearin' man. I jes' wish he wouldn't make all o' us git down an' pray WITH him! I know he'd call me A Sinner headin' straight fer Hell, an' mebbe that's right. But fact is, an' to call it out plain, I don't know if I kin TAKE much more prayin'!'

Sturgill said, 'Well, I'm 'bout half-way to your side. He's been through a lot. But *that man has got more religion…than I can rightly ABIDE!*'

The next morning, they waded the Creek, swollen and muddy with the recent rain, and within a quarter mile had entered the water Gap, a dramatic gorge that the river had sliced through Pine Mountain…a ridge just as long, just as high, and just as rocky, as Cumberland Mountain. They followed The Trace, the river on their right hand. Their spirits were lifted when they passed three tiny cabins perched beside the riverbank. Two were unoccupied. But an old woman was sitting in front of the last one, and greeted them.

'Welcome to Kaintuck! This here is Th' Narrers. Jes' a mile! JES' ONE MORE MILE! to Th' Ford. But look out fer them rocks on top o' th' Mountain!'

The Narrows was a perfect name, as the Gap WAS exceedingly narrow, perhaps no more than a few hundred feet wide in places. Huge sandstone boulders loomed high above, some situated so precariously it was not unreasonable to imagine they might fall at any moment.

'Look out fer them rocks! They is TREMENJOUS big. They might likely fall down an' crush youun's to DEATH!' She laughed loudly…she even slapped her thigh…as though this was absolutely the FUNNIEST story anyone had EVER told. 'Now you look out fer them rocks, you hear?'

As they exited the water gap, the Trace curved round a bend where a creek entered the river. They now saw how river and creek functioned…the river draining the South slope of Pine Mountain, the creek draining the North slope. At the bend of the river was a broad floodplain, dotted with clearings and tents. Nine groups of Settlers, some forty people in all, were camped beside The Ford, waiting for the water level to subside. The river, swollen by the recent rain, was much too high for people or animals to wade.

'Hit's goin' down…goin' down purty fast. Might be ford-able tomorrer, or day a'ter tomorrer. Fer sartin', th' day a'ter that.' They found a clearing and pitched camp. There was pasture, scant but perhaps enough, for their animals. Sturgill noted that some Settlers had brought cattle and hogs, even chickens in baskets, and realized that he and Tolbert had made a mistake in leaving their livestock behind. Mayme and Hannah helped Sturgill's wife make hoecake, and Hargis cleaned his rifle so he'd be ready to hunt at dawn. Settlers told him, 'They's plenty o' game, but ye got to git away from th' river. Go up th' mountain, back up th' holler.' He heard a fiddle and clapping, and saw children dancing. *Something to do.*

The next day, Hargis returned toward sundown with two turkeys, and their group feasted. He made the circuit of the other campfires, picking up information. One man ventured, 'This ain't th' best land in Kaintuck. Valleys an' hollers is all narrer, but th' creek bottoms is rich. If yer fixin' to jes' farm fer yourse'f, livin' mainly off game, this might be as good a place as th' next. I hear nobobody's entered th' land up Marrowbone Creek yonder.'

Hargis thought this important information, and was formulating more questions. But just then Mayme tugged at his sleeve and whispered in his ear. Hargis looked startled, and the two of them went off alone into the woods.

The next morning, Mayme was whispering again, this time to Sturgill's wife. She sat still, looking straight ahead, her face stony. She scarcely moved for ten minutes…just stirring the pot. Then she whispered to her husband.

After the noon dinner, Sturgill said, 'Looks like th' tide is past an' th' river's droppin' fast. Folks say we kin git 'cross Th' Ford tomorrer.' Then he pulled Tolbert aside. The two men went off together. When they returned, their expressions were somber.

Tolbert assembled the group, and spoke slowly, gravely. 'Sturgill says Mayme tole his wife she's missed her monthly flux…an' is sick ever' mornin'. She says hit is sartin'…Mayme is With Child.'

Tolbert's skin was the color of gray flint, and his jaw was locked in grim determination. 'God hates Sin! But God FORGIVES Th' Sinner! Amen! Praise be to God Almighty!' He paused, breathing hard.

'Mayme! Git out here! Hargis, YOU boy! Git out here! You sneak off…fornicatin'…makin' a baby? What do ye plan to DO, Boy? How ye 'spect to git Right with God? How kin ye wash away yer Sin?…An' YOU, Mayme, what would yer Maw say?' Tolbert shed no tears and made no threats. But his face made clear he had no idea at all what to do next.

Sturgill broke the tension. 'Frazer, this ain't what none of us woulda' wanted. Maybe hit is A Sin. But Mayme is a hard worker, an' she is Old Enough. Hargis kin hunt bettern' you an' me put together. Why not just let 'em marry right here an' now? Ain't that fer th' best?'

Tolbert had said less and less since his wife died. He now seemed at a total loss, what to say, what to do...He looked as though he might faint. He fell on both knees, bowed his head, and prayed. 'Lord, You have seen us through to Kaintuck, an' we're boun' now to *cross over* to th' good land in New Zion. We thank Ye fer Yore Blessing. If hit be Yore Will, bless this Woman an' her baby that's comin'...an' her husbin'. We ast it in Jesus' name. AMEN!'

He rose painfully to his feet. He looked and moved like an old, old man.

'Sturgill says there ain't no Preacher here. But GOD is A Preacher...th' Best Preacher. He kin bless you, if ye aim to git Right with Him. Sturgill, ye'll jist have to do somethin'! *I cain't go on!*'

Tolbert stood unsteadily, bewildered. He moved away and pretended to spy something high up on the mountainside, anything to avert his gaze.

Sturgill's wife went into the tent and brought out Tolbert's Bible and handed it to her husband. The two of them held The Book, its pages open. She and her husband placed Mayme's hand and Hargis' hand atop The Book. Sturgill's eyes darted all around. He was earnestly seeking HELP. But he was alone. He would have to say SOMEthing...but his mind was a total BLANK.

'Mayme, you an' Hargis have made a baby. D'ye think maybe that might be God's way o' makin' up fer yer Maw's death...? An' fer th' little baby that died? If ye two say you'uns want to be Married, an' ye say it right now, then we'un's will agree, an' we'uns will say, that you IS Married from now on.'

Tolbert's four boys laughed and made faces, and Hannah blushed beet red. Mayme started giggling and seemed unable to stop. Hargis mumbled 'Yes.'

Tolbert watched from a distance, then came back and addressed Sturgill. 'I'm a-gon'a jine up with this bunch here at Th' Ford. We're headin' to Boone's Fort. We has come a good ways, an' we are in Kaintuck. We are IN GOD'S HANDS. He has A Plan. He will decide.' He went into the woods alone.

By dawn the next day the river had fallen and the rocky bottom could be seen clearly. All agreed the water was now so low the river could be safely waded even by children. Tolbert and his four boys stood next to Hargis. Mayme and Hannah held hands and mumbled farewells. Mayme kissed her father on the cheek. Tolbert intended to pray, but found himself speechless. His voice failed…no sound at all. His lips could not form words. Hargis and Mayme heard…maybe, perhaps…'God Bless' and 'Luck.'

Settlers packed quickly. By noon almost all had crossed The Ford. The Trace turned north to Flat Lick, and the horses were soon out of sight.

Ten minutes later Tolbert's oldest boy came running back. He was panting hard, completely out of breath.

He held up three fingers:

'NUMBER ONE: Paw sez 'Pray to God and He will bless you'.'

'NUMBER TWO: Paw sez 'Keep th' rifle'.'

'NUMBER THREE: 'He sez, 'Keep th' axe'.'

Sturgill came up to Hargis, with a stranger by his side. 'This here is John Bledsoe. He sez he's heered too much bad about Fort Boone to go thar.'

Bledsoe added, 'An' I jes' don't have no mind to trek with Tolbert. Feller's got jes' *TOO DAMN MUCH GOD FER ME!* I'll git to Heaven my own way or mebbe I jist won't GO!' This prompted Bledsoe to emit a long stream of brown tobacco juice.

'I rode up Marrowbone Creek yonder.' He gestured toward a narrow valley shrouded in thick morning mist. 'Game all over. Good water. Poplar, hickory, oak, chestnut, plenty o' mast. Bottom land in th' hollers. I got two growed sons. I think mebbe ye could live good up thar. No mucky-mucks up thar to bother ye. I'll head up that a-ways with you'uns…if ye want.'

The three groups chose narrow side valleys five miles apart. That was as much proximity as they could tolerate, even neighbors that might help them. *Kaintuck meant freedom.* That was why they left the group at The Ford. That was why they chose to settle many miles AWAY from The Trace…as far back as possible…at the extreme head of the most remote hollers.

The first year was the hardest, as they had little desire to work together. But necessity forced them…By pooling tools and muscles, each had completed by June a tiny rough cabin. The sight of blue smoke curling up from each other's chimneys was as close as they wanted. Each then cleared his particular patch…felling every tree for acres around, and burning all the stumps. After rocks were cleared, the women and children planted corn. The men were mostly gone, off in the woods, hunting game for food…and for hides and pelts to trade for seeds, black powder and lead, cloth and thread, copper for a still.

With Sturgill's Old Woman beside her, Mayme's baby was born in December 1779. Hargis named him Robert. He had Mayme's red hair, blue eyes, and pale white complexion. Another good omen: Bledsoe's stallion and Hargis' mare produced a strong foal, which, in the spring of 1780, Hargis traded for a heifer and some pigs. People were talking…that The Trace might be improved so wagons could carry goods to and from Kaintuck.

In September 1780, his wife and children busy shucking corn, Sturgill decided this might be a good time to ride back to Watauga for his livestock.

As Sturgill stopped at Inns and Trading Posts along the way, Rumor became Fact: 'What has Th' King ever' done for Th' Poor Man, 'cept hang 'im?! Now th' British is armin' Injuns, urgin' 'em to scalp ever' Settler, a Pound fer ev'ry white scalp. Us mountain men, Watauga, Kaintuck, eve'whar, cain't jes' SIT if we aim to stay FREE! Hit's WAR in Carolina! Tories is fightin' fer th' King, Patriots is fightin' fer Freedom. Tarleton's Legion an' Major Ferguson is killin' ALL Th' Patriots! *Wipin' 'em out! We're doomed TOO if'n we don' he'p 'em!'*

Sturgill joined nine hundred Over Mountain Men at Sycamore Shoals, with more joining as the column rode south. Sturgill had known Isaac Shelby, leader of the Watauga militia, and chose to ride with him. Shelby led untamed backwoodsmen with no military discipline whatever, mainly 'out fer revenge.' George Rogers Clark's victory at Vincennes in 1779 prevented the British from driving Americans from the western frontier. And The Battle of King's Mountain, followed by the brutal mopping-up, turned the tide in the South.

Sturgill was killed October 7, 1780, at King's Mountain. It was weeks before word reached Marrowbone Creek. In December, Colonel Shelby arrived at The Ford to claim, by authority of Virginia Military Warrant, a four hundred acre Section for himself. Sturgill's Widow was awarded, by Warrant, two hundred acres. Sturgill's son Ambrose, sixteen, took over the hunting…and his Mother and the younger children hoed the corn patch.

The cabin occupied by Hargis, Mayme and their baby in the winter of 1780-81 was identical to all mountain cabins that were built in great haste…its stick chimney framed of green laths, its flue plastered inside with thick mud. Hargis gathered stones and 'determined' he would build a better chimney 'come spring.' But on a freezing night in February 1781, the chimney caught fire. The blaze spread to the roof, and fire had engulfed the cabin before Hargis and Mayme were roused from sleep. Hargis battled the flames while Mayme gathered up their baby, now a toddler…but in doing so, her clothing caught fire…and she was horribly burned.

Mayme died in early March 1781 of 'Fever.'

Sturgill's Widow cared for Hargis' son, Robert, now eighteen months old. Hargis did not rebuild the cabin.

Spring breathed life into the stark skeletons of trees, and the woods were infused with a rain-fresh shimmering light, ferns unfurling from tight fiddleheads into trembling green feathers.

Hargis found that hunting did not relieve his sorrow, but he welcomed the isolation. He needed TIME. In May, he began to hunt in an area he had never seen before. As he followed the creek up the mountain, the stream became increasingly narrow…until near the crest, there was no water at all. He urged his horse on. A quarter-mile further, and he began to descend, following another stream…this one flowing to the north. Other branches joined, and after a few miles he was in the bed of a wide creek, his horse's hooves cooled by a strong flow of clear water, the creek teeming with fish and frogs. Yellow-bellied sapsuckers drilled into the trees, and in the warm May sun pale green leaves emerged from winter buds.

He came to a clearing, every tree felled or burned, and saw smoke from a weathered cabin, a sure sign someone must be near. He greeted the two women sitting in front, the yard bare of grass, swept clean with twig brooms.

'How do folks call this-here part o' th' country?'

Lilah Begley and her daughter Maggie, both smoking stained cob pipes, had the mountaineer's innate wariness…But hospitality finally won out.

'Howdy-do? How's weather up yore way? Kin we give ye some water?' Hargis accepted, and drank from their long-stemmed gourd.

'This here is Red Bird. Some say Red Bird Creek, some say Red Bird River. I don't rightly know where it comes out…. My Old Man's out huntin', always out huntin', that's what he does,' said Lilah. 'My boy

Mason's with him. They might be back by dark. We never know fer sure. You're welcome to set.'

After filling his pipe and sharing some berries picked along the way, Hargis told his story…all of it…Ulster, to Plantation, to Wilderness Road. But when he came to the death of his wife Mayme, he was unable to stifle his tears. Lilah and her daughter both reached out, touching his sleeve.

Lilah said, 'We have it mighty HARD back here! MIGHTY hard! But we-un's is TOUGH. We kin make it!' She accented this with puffs on her pipe. 'You 'pears to be a fine strong young man. You kin make it…*SARTIN*!' Maggie said, 'I shore am sorry to hear 'bout yore Wife…An' 'bout yore Baby that's got no Maw…'

Simon Begley and his son Mason returned at sundown. After comment on the 'unusual weather,' the three men got down to the all-important subject…*hunting*. 'Bear an' elk sure is mighty scase nowadays. An' jes' a few gobblers. Folks hereabouts is livin' mostly off deer an' squirrel-meat.'

That point settled, it was time to get out Black Betty. By the time all three had enjoyed several long pulls on the jug and had filled their pipes, the sun had gone behind the hill. Lilah brought out a kettle of squirrel-meat that had been stewing since dawn, and they ate by the dim light of the hearth. Hargis accepted their offer to stay, 'If'n I kin jes' make a pallet on th' floor.'

Two months later Hargis announced that Maggie had agreed to be his Old Woman. This was the signal for a two-day celebration, during which Simon got so drunk he fell and broke his nose. But the accident didn't slow him down, and he continued to fire his rifle into the air all the next day. Lilah said the new configuration of his nose improved his appearance considerably.

Their son James was born in 1783…straight black hair and swarthy skin…not as dark as Maggie's…nor half as dark as Lilah's.

Hargis selected a holler with a clear spring that flowed steadily from beneath a ledge. Simon Begley and his son Mason, and John Bledsoe and his two sons came to help with a *workings*. They rode over the watershed and camped for a week on Red Bird River. They felled huge poplars that were pulled to the clearing by Hargis' mare. The logs were set on stone piers, ends hewed to a tight half-dovetail notch with axes, wedges, froe, auger and maul. The single-pen cabin had one door leading to the front of the clearing, two hinged windows on each side. Gaps between the logs were tightly chinked inside and out, then daubed wind-tight with clay. Chestnut logs were shaved flat for puncheon floors, and pegs in the walls held clothing. The cabin was roofed with split oak shingles set on skinned poles. There was enough height for a sleeping loft above the room, with tiny windows in each gable end. Bedsteads laced with sinew ropes and corn shucks or feather beds would do just fine for children certain to appear. The good-drawing stone chimney was used for cooking and heating. The stones were set in burnt limestone and sand. The men agreed it was solid.

When the cabin was finished, Hargis and Maggie walked over the crest, then down Marrowbone Creek to the clearing of Widow Sturgill, returning with Robert, who had Mayme's Scots-Irish coloration, reddish hair, blue eyes, pale complexion…in striking contrast to James, who had Maggie's black hair, black eyes, and copper coloration. Hargis and Maggie had six more children, only two of which survived to adulthood. Everyone called their holler 'Maggie's Branch'…for a simple reason. The river was named for Chief Red Bird. Maggie was part Cherokee. Could she have been Red Bird's daughter? Who knew? 'Maggie's Branch' it was. A generation later, Hargis joined with others to make a cemetery and build a one-room log schoolhouse.

Every year Hargis felled more trees, burnt stumps, removed rocks…clearing, grubbing, hoeing. He used a bull-tongue plow pulled by his mare, aging but still strong. His main crop was corn. Every so often he and Maggie filled jute poke sacks with shelled corn, loading their animals, more numerous since Hargis' brood mare had produced two more colts, for the trip to the Mill. Hargis split chestnut logs for rail fencing and also made chairs and tables. They raised hay and fodder for their horses, and for a cow and heifer. They had pear, plum and cherry trees, and grew cabbage, potatoes, turnips, onions, a little tobacco. Pawpaws, blackberries, and huckleberries were abundant, as was sassafras for tea. Sheep dotted the pastures, and Maggie used walnut hulls and sumac to dye the wool she spun, some mixed with flax into linsey-woolsey. They obtained honey from bee gums, and sweet syrup from boiling the juice of sorghum cane. Chickens and guinea fowl roosted in the trees, and geese controlled insects in the corn patch, and provided down for bed ticks and pillows. Shoat pigs ran wild in the woods, growing fat on chestnut and oak mast. Late fall and winter was hog-killing time, the meat salted and preserved, the fat rendered into lard or used for soap. They made most everything they needed, a labor that kept them all, even the children, working every hour of daylight, so busy they had no time to notice their isolation. What little they could not make…shoes, some cloth and thread and needles, salt and coffee, kettles, iron for horseshoes and tools, copper for a whiskey coil…were obtained by trapping and trading game pelts, or trading herbs like ginseng, yellow-root, witch hazel, galax, golden-seal, and bloodroot. They spent much time outdoors, grubbing corn, or hunting. Indoors, the cabin hearth was the center of their lives. Gourds, dried limber twig and berry red apples, strings of shucky beans grown between corn rows, strips of Cushaw squash, pumpkin, and squirrel and venison…dried in the chimney smoke.

For hunting, Hargis used the rifle Frazer Tolbert had given him, although he increasingly relied on traps, as they required no powder or lead. He was aided by the enthusiastic baying of four mangy hounds, usually asleep in the dirt under the cabin, fed on rabbits or groundhogs. His proudest possession, his only worthy possession, was Gilley's old rifle, its maple stock polished and gleaming. It hung above the hearth, atop a six-point antler-rack...elk now impossible to find...the rifle turned so the old mark was visible:

WG
1768

THE MILLER
ROBERT BROUGHTON,
1779–1845

◆

It took weeks for word to reach Marrowbone Creek. But when Widow Sturgill learned that Colonel Isaac Shelby had, on June 4, 1792, been sworn in as Kentucky's first Governor, she knew what to do. She sent word to her son Ambrose, 28. He now lived two hollers over, had cleared fifty acres and burned off fifty more, had built a cabin, smokehouse and corncrib, owned a cow and hogs, and was married with three children, a fourth on the way.

'Ambrose, you know 'sgood as me that yore daddy rode with Colonel Shelby at King's Mountain, an' it was Shelby that give us this land. He's now Governor of th' entire STATE! Ain't that SOMETHIN'! I cain't say pre-zackly why...an' maybe it's jes' a fool thang...But I'd shorely like ye to ride over t' Danville t' see 'im. D'ye think it might take two days over, two days back? I hear tell he's got a fine big house. Jes' say we are mighty grateful he 'membered yore Paw, an' by givin' us this land he he'ped us go on a'ter yer Paw was kilt.'

'Kin ye do that?' Ambrose's face made clear he wasn't happy about this strange mission, but finally nodded agreement.

'An don't fergit to tell him,' his Mother added, 'How might PLEASED all o' us in Marrowbone Creek is, that he is our Governor!'

When Ambrose returned, he reported 'A Big Mob' at Shelby's estate, Traveler's Rest. By dint of strong elbows, he managed to squeeze inside, shake the Governor's hand, and deliver his Mother's message.

'Colonel Shelby is a powerful STOUT man, so big you cain't hardly get close to him! They was people on all sides, in front o' him, in back o' him, hollerin', all wantin' jobs, wantin' this, wantin' that. An' ever' one of 'em said they was at King's Mountain with Th' Colonel. I cain't deposit how he could have airy idea who I might be. But when I said *'I'm th' son o' Virgil Sturgill'*...ever'body just bust a gut LAUGHIN'! But Th' Colonel shut 'em up quick! He said 'Sturgill was my fren', an' 'He was A Patriot who gave his life for this New Country. Nobody durst laugh at his Boy!'...An' then I thanked him, like you said to do, an' left.'

In 1797 the Kentucky Legislature appropriated five hundred pounds for repair of The Wilderness Road. To raise money for upkeep, they authorized a Toll Gate at The Narrows. Ambrose was at a Camp Meeting near Flat Lick and had just been *saved*...when he heard The Big News...*The Kentucky Road would be kept passable by wagons*! The Preacher, anxious to help A New Soul For Christ, wrote a letter for him, asking Shelby if Ambrose could be considered for the post of Tollgate Keeper. The Camp Meeting was also where Ambrose acquired a Bible in exchange for two pigs. The Preacher spent four days showing him how, slowly, laboriously, to sound out *The Word*.

A few weeks later Ambrose received news that he had been awarded the job...a position that gave him the best possible vantage point to witness one of the most amazing migrations in American history. Perhaps three hundred thousand settlers...had ALREADY followed The Road. But the flow was not abating...in fact, numbers seemed to increase. Most days he welcomed, and collected from, a score or more. Most were families lured by stories of The New Eden. They knew that years of hard work lay ahead. They knew they were dependent on game until they had cleared and planted and harvested. But almost all were young, animated by a fierce desire to better their lot. The forest would provide timber for cabin, corncrib, smokehouse, stable, fencing. The forest would become pasture and cropland. The cycle of poverty their fathers had endured would be ended. Land would set them free. Land would allow them to determine their own destiny. They would be independent...Free Men...beholden to no one.

Ambrose quickly realized that his job entailed some Big Problems. The State was to receive all fees collected, according to the following schedule:

ACT FOR A ROAD TO THE GAP

'The keeper of the turnpike shall be entitled to receive the following toll: each person, except post riders, expresses and women and children under the age of ten years, nine-pence; every horse, mare or mule, nine-pence; every carriage with two wheels, three shillings; every carriage with four wheels, six shillings; every head of meat cattle going east-ward, three pence. Each head of hogs 1/2 cent; each head of sheep 1/5 cent; each vehicle drawn by one horse or mule, 20 cents; by two horses or mules, 25 cents; each wagon drawn by three horses, mules, or oxen, 30 cents; each stage coach with seats inside for six passengers, 35 cents.'

Many travelers could not understand why they should pay *ANYTHING at all!* Some flatly REFUSED, resulting in long heated discussions, and much abuse hurled at Ambrose. Many of those WILLING to pay, had no money of any kind. So he began to improvise...accepting payment-in-kind rather than coin...things like fat hens, bushels of apples, baskets of vegetables, livestock, whatever travelers thought they could do without. (A few were drovers herding cattle, hogs, and sometimes as many as five hundred turkeys in a gang, driven to Virginia for sale to the great tobacco and cotton plantations.) He began to keep a Ledger, soliciting help from those able to write. Ambrose paid the State in cash, but gave himself a little bonus on every in-kind transaction. Each bonus was tiny, but over time...he acquired more hens, hogs, cattle and horses than anyone in Marrowbone Creek. He also began to acquire a bad reputation. That did not worry him one bit. He was *saved*. He was now *A Christian Man*. God would tell him what to do. *Under God's protection, he could do no wrong.*

Ambrose had been at The Toll Gate day-in day-out for nine years, except for three furloughs a year for planting, harvesting, and hog butchering. By this time he had accumulated a fair quantity of livestock, and his expanding acreage of grazing land and cropland was neatly enclosed with split-chestnut fencing. His neighbors considered him wealthy. He began to ponder seriously how he might use his good fortune.

At his Mother's urging, he sent a letter to Shelby asking if The Colonel might want to sell the four hundred acres of bottom land he had acquired in the winter of 1780-81. Shelby had never occupied the land, nor had he farmed it. Would he perhaps like to sell? Shelby replied, but set a VERY steep price...five dollars per acre...but 'Because you are Sturgis' Boy, I trust you. Pay me over five years, one-fifth per year.' Ambrose did not have even a fraction of this much cash, nor any idea how he might get it, though he thought his livestock might be worth half that much. He wrote back accepting the terms.

By now, nineteen cabins were perched along the bank between The Cumberland River and The Wilderness Road...strung out a mile, from the Tollgate at The Narrows...to The Ford. The cabins were occupied by people profiting one way or another off travelers: a forge and blacksmith, a stable selling oats and meal, a cabin selling smoked hog-meat and berries in season, and several cabins where one could buy jugs of whiskey...or a loose woman.

Ambrose thought he had seen it all. But on a raw blustery February morning in 1806, he was jolted awake by the strangest caravan that had ever passed his Gate. In the lead was a two-horse phaeton, driven by a black boy dressed in good clothing. Seated beside him was a pale-complected white man of perhaps forty, dressed in black suit-and-vest and a white shirt with gold collar-button, no necktie. Seated behind was a homely matron, dressed also in black, and a girl of uncertain age but certainly younger than twenty. The both wore sunbonnets of good cloth.

Lumbering behind were two ENORMOUS wagons, heavily loaded with plows, hoes, and every other kind of farm implement, and overflowing with wooden crates and trunks. The front wagon was driven by a black man, about thirty, handling the reins of a four-mule team; the second was driven by a somewhat older black man, handling the reins of a four-ox team, large red shorthorn steers, plodding slowly. No Settler had EVER passed with this much gear...two adult slaves, one teenage slave (and two black women and perhaps six black children), two horses, four mules, four oxen. Ambrose had never before seen such an *incredible* amount of ***ROLLING WEALTH.***

While he was mentally calculating The Toll (he thought these daily calculations helped him read better), the black-suited man got down from his carriage. He appeared of average size when sitting high up. But when he was on the ground, Ambrose saw he was just over five feet tall, and weighed perhaps a hundred ten pounds wringing wet. He wore a white hat of very fine, tightly woven straw, of a type Ambrose had never seen before. Gold-framed pince-nez glasses were delicately perched on his beak of a nose. A port-wine birthmark ran down the left side of his face, a streak of jagged red lightning.

Ambrose said, 'We sure is mighty PLEASED to see you here in Kaintuck. You must be a good farmer with such fine animals an' so much gear.'

'I am not A Farmer...' The man paused for effect...'I am A Planter.'

The Planter's thick Virginia accent, and his manner of accenting words, made him sound like an oral version of a red-letter Bible. He pointed to the black men at the reins of the carriage and two Wagons: 'Wash and Jeff are THE FARMERS. The soil over in Floyd County GAVE OUT! Not worth any thing! NOTHING! No Planter even made back the SEED! We are looking to spy out some GOOD land over this way.'

The stranger stuck out his hand, 'I am Carter Jackson. And you ARE?'

'Ambrose Sturgill. Mighty pleased t' meet ye. If'n ye kin tell me whar ye-all is a-headin', I might kin give ye some idea o' how to git thar…'

'Well, I want GOOD LAND. Everybody in Virginia I talked to said that there is a vast ABUNDANCE of rich, fertile land just about every-where in Kentucky…all of it FAR better than our worn-out tobacco land in Virginia. I plant burley tobacco for cash…oats for the horses and mules…corn for the hogs and negras…and fruit trees and vegeta-bles for my wife and daughter.'

Jackson nodded again toward his slaves. 'I simply HAVE TO make a good crop! It is my DUTY! The Bible says 'God cursed the sons of Ham.' But I am A CHRISTIAN man, and I have prayed to God…And He answered: 'Look after the negras, even though they ARE cursed! Most people have no idea at all what *A HEAVY BURDEN* it is to look after negras! You've got to feed them, clothe them, tell them what to do and when to do it, and give them a cabin. Even if they are lazy and will NOT work, you are still STUCK with them! It is a heavy, HEAVY burden! But with God's help, I will go on. *I Will Bear The Burden*!'

The allusions to God and God's Will prompted Ambrose to reveal that he was *saved*. While The Planter's slaves fetched buckets of water for the animals, The Planter and Ambrose discussed a few points of theology.

'I've got God's Holy Word right here,' said Ambrose, pulling out his Bible. 'An' I'm doin' ever' thang I kin to read hit. But hit's mighty HARD!'

'Well, if I had enough time, I might be able to help you. It's the most important thing in the world, reading The Word of God. I read The Bible every single day…I don't EVER fail!…And I pray. Do you pray EVERY DAY?'

'Oh yes! An' Th' Word's a Comfort if people cuss at me 'bout The Toll.'

The Planter reached into his black vest and pulled out a heavy gold watch, firmly attached by an equally heavy gold chain. He flipped open the gold lid and squinted through his pince-nez at the dial. 'Well, I made a promise to God that I would pray at Sunrise, at Noon, and at Sunset. It's about five minutes to Noon, Virginia Time. Would you excuse me for moment?' And with that, The Planter walked a few paces away and bowed his head, mumbling quietly. Then he said an audible 'Amen!' and returned.

Ambrose's brain was racing feverishly. 'Well, Kaintuck is shorely th' BESTEST PLACE…if yer lookin' fer real good farm land. 'Course you want to take yer time, look ever'thing over, make sure hit's right fer ye.'

Ambrose appraised The Virginia Planter, attempting calculations in his head…but his brain was simply unable to count up such a staggering sum. 'Now, it jes' so happens I do know 'bout a might' fine section o' bottom land. Soil so rich ye kin eat it with a spoon! Butter! Ye kin grow ANY thang on lan' like THAT! An' hit's jes' one mile up th' road…An' hit's mighty CHEAP, too! Jes' ten dollars an acre! Cain't beat it!…Bes' land!…Bes' price!…ANY whar in Kaintuck!'

The Planter said, 'Well, I have HEARD that the best tobacco land in the FLAT part of the State has been CLAIMED. But no harm in just A LOOK, eh?'

After two weeks of minute inspection of the land Shelby had acquired and sold, and after long palaver…Carter Jackson, Virginia Planter and Man of Property…and Ambrose Sturgill, Wilderness Road Tollgate Tender [and would-be Man of Property], shook hands.

Ambrose could not believe it! *ALL CASH!* He was transformed in a moment from poverty to wealth. He was rich! He realized instantly that this windfall was *A Seed that could grow into A Fortune.* He succumbed instantly to a severe case of THE VIRGINIA DISEASE. Ambrose resolved then and there to buy more land, more than he could ever possibly plow, buy slaves to farm it for him, rent land to tenants, and buy still MORE! An' MORE after THAT!…'Land's the only thing that lasts…I might OWN these mountains!'

The Planter and The Tollgate Keeper undertook another transaction in the Spring of 1807 when Ambrose's son, Homer Sturgill, 22, wed The Planter's daughter, Nancy Jackson, 20…The Reverend Zophar Asher, a circuit-riding acolyte of Wesley's *Method*, presiding. The parson would accept only a tiny fee…'on condition that the two Families hereby Joined promise to build A Chapel.' The Reverend, The Planter, Ambrose Sturgill, and the Two Newlyweds, prayed together…then Shook Hands. It was a solemn moment.

'People up Marrowbone Creek,' thought Robert Broughton, who had moved over the watershed after a quarrel with his brother James, 'Are plum wore-out.' Several times a season they had to load wagons with their shelled corn, make the trip to The Mill…'All of a day to get there, then wait a turn jes' to get your corn ground'…then try to make it back before dark, possible only during the long days of summer. Most seasons you had to sleep in The Mill after sundown. There was good gossip. 'But taking everything together, having to trek so far is a plain dadgum BOTHER, is what it is.'

'An' everybody says The Miller *keeps too much!*'

It bothered Robert, too…but he saw a solution. Broughton walked all over his Holler, sketching in his mind where things might go. His Branch had a strong flow in every season, and old-timers said it never went dry. There was a good head, water dropping swiftly down to The Creek. He could build the Dam upstream here, broad space behind for a large Millpond, perhaps even with fish. The Headgate and Race-channel could run along here, the Tailrace could flow back to The Branch this way. He would control the Flume by boards and a Waterbox. If he sited The Mill *here*…water from the Flume would be high enough to turn an efficient and powerful overshot Wheel. At the head of the holler was *the building material*…enormous white oaks, pale gray bark mottled with blue-green lichen, branches draped with mistletoe, the litter thick with acorns, mushrooms, fungi, puffballs, galls and oak apples…saw flies buzzing softly as they circled the foxglove.

He had The Water. He had The Oak. But he needed Cash…enough, as a minimum, for ironwork and Millstones. There was ONE possibility. Carter Jackson's wagons permitted him to transport his hogsheads of tobacco to market in Virginia. He also rented his wagons, teams, and slaves…which brought in more cash. He had also installed a rope ferry across The Ford, since he owned the southern bank anyway. The Ferry was not a big moneymaker, but the income was steady. All this enabled him to build The Jackson-Sturgill Chapel at The Narrows, buy more draft animals and wagons and harness, and furnish his home with luxury items so rare as to seem from another world.

The Planter received him warmly in his two-story house, the largest structure between Cumberland Gap and Flat Lick. It was sited atop the ancient Indian burial mound, thus well above the spring floods, silty tides that enriched his crops with humus from both slopes of Pine Mountain. The House On The Mound was built of poplar logs felled on Governor Shelby's Warrant section. All the trees on this once thickly timbered acreage had been felled, and it was now entirely cropland and pasture. The exterior logs had been hewed and whitewashed in a most workmanlike manner by his slaves, the cozy interior sheathed with painted clapboard. It was a virtual Virginia Plantation in a place known only a few decades before as 'The Wilderness.'

The Planter listened intently. 'I think you are correct about the need for a grist Mill. I myself have been TROUBLED by long trips simply to get my oats and corn milled. And having seen my negras SWEAT in a

whipsaw pit making clapboards for this house, I think there might be
GOOD PROFIT in a Sawmill, too. But building A Mill is a very serious
enterprise. *Serious!* VERY serious! Takes considerable knowledge, time,
energy, MONEY. And EXPERIENCE! Most of all, you need *experience!*
You have to KNOW what you are ABOUT! I have seen Mills built by
ignorant people…and through TRIAL-AND-ERROR they sometimes
work…'

'…But more often…they BREAK DOWN!' His face made exceedingly clear his firm conviction that trial-and-error was STUPID…and
that EXPERIENCE had his unqualified approbation.

'Everybody tells me you are strong, intelligent, ambitious. Talking
with you here today, I agree most HEARTILY with that opinion. You
seem a fine capable fellow! Outstanding reputation! BUT WITHOUT
EXPERIENCE, going it alone, there is NO HOPE OF SUCCESS!
Building A Mill requires a good knowledge of mathematics. And you
can't BEGIN to plan until you have good burrstones. Everything has to
be thought-out in advance, calculated, so it FITS. When everything fits
together, a Mill works like a well-regulated WATCH!'

This *word* was, of course, his cue to extract his massive gold time-
piece, open its thick lid, and peer through his curious spectacles at the
dial…He was entirely aware…that the action emphasized his Point.

'When I was planting tobacco back in Virginia, we were FORTU-
NATE to have a first-class Millwright there in Floyd County…Buford
Logan…Logan has built at least A DOZEN mills all over southwest
Virginia.'

He gazed distantly at the mountains from his window…a proper
window with GLASS…the only glass 'winders' within ten miles of The
Gap.

'I will go this far with you: I will DISPATCH Wash to Virginia with a
wagonload of tobacco. I will also give him A LETTER to post. If Logan
can be FOUND, I will INVITE him to come through The Gap, and be
my GUEST here at The Ford. This gentleman is An Expert. After he has

EXAMINED what you have in mind, and after we have *reasoned together*, perhaps we can AGREE?'

Buford Logan, Millwright, arrived at The Ford in October 1822, and stayed three weeks. With Carter Jackson and Robert Broughton beside him, he rode up and down Marrowbone Creek once a day for five days running. He paced out the length and breadth of various sites. At some, he drew maps with gradient lines. He examined many Branches and Creeks, and at some he used a folding yard-stick…six feet, twelve feet…measuring The Fall of the water, though he was quick to warn that this was a preliminary Estimate. He brought a few surveying instruments that helped suggest where a Millpond could be sited, and the Quantity of water it could contain. He talked at length with Bill Crabtree, Smith, at The Forge in The Narrows, and examined his work…to ascertain if he had the skill to fabricate bearings and gear teeth.

Eight days elapsed before they rode up Marrowbone Creek again. But The Millwright had not been idle. He was, rather, laboring mentally in The Planter's Office…drawing and calculating. Broughton noticed that he seemed to base his arithmetic on Tables found in a well-thumbed book. When The Planter wasn't around, Broughton saw its title…*The Young Mill-Wright & Miller's Guide*, by Oliver Evans.

Toward the end of the second week, the three rode several times up and down Marrowbone Creek, The Millwright making more precise measurements. At his Branch, the very site Broughton himself thought might be most likely, he wrote down the most numbers. *Broughton owned that entire holler!*

At the end of the third week, Broughton, The Millwright, and The Planter sat down…to 'Reason Together.'

The Millwright did most of the talking. 'People will tell you that good Mill Stones must be imported from France. Not so! They are making good-cutting burr stones at a quarry on Brush Mountain…Uncle Zack

Price owns the mill rock pits, a section patented by Colonel Patton…about halfway between Wolf Hills and Great Lick.'

'I think I KNOW the place,' said The Planter. 'About three days' ride.'

'They have been working the pits there for twenty years, and have the rock pretty well figured out now. It is extremely hard sandstone, tiny glass pebbles embedded within it. It is the glass edge of the pebbles that does the cutting. They read each stone, then blast with black powder to crack them on the grain. They dress the stones with wedges, cutting and block hammers, chisels, pitching tools.'

'Of course those tools must be made from good English steel, not pig iron. They temper their tools by color…not cherry red, but the color of gray straw…and they know when and how to quench. They sharpen every day. The hardest part is holding the bull set at the right angle so it cuts, doesn't skid off, and doesn't take too much off. They know how to face the runner and bedstone, make them both flat and level. They know where to put the furrows, how many, and what kind of edge. Oh, it is an extremely specialized trade, quite skilled, and not just anybody can do it. Putting in the eye is the delicate part, round eye for the runner stone, square eye for the bedstone. Stone that hard is brittle, and some times it just falls apart. And you need box-holes in back of the stone, so you can add lead. They put it on a spud, turn it, melt lead, and add weight till it turns nice and level. They make stones for shelling oats, hulling buckwheat, grinding middlings, hemp, tanbark, apple pomace. You can even grind snuff…with the right stone. But I assume you plan mainly to grind corn and oats…eh?'

The Planter was fascinated, but from his point of view they had made *no progress at all.* 'Now Mr. Broughton, The Millwright here says your holler and branch MIGHT DO nicely. Your Branch has a strong FLOW and a high HEAD. But there is the COST of Millstones, and the COST of transporting them. We will need a Smith and good IRONWORK here at The Ford. Then there is the COST of a sash saw from a forge in Virginia. And we must COMPENSATE our Expert Millwright'…and

The Planter nodded in a courtly Virginia-Gentleman way toward
Buford Logan…'This planning trip now…Then he must return and
supervise construction. We might OWE HIM three months' WAGE! We
also have to CALCULATE how much timber, of what kind, and how it is
to be hewed. We have to CALCULATE how to build the Millpond Dam
and Raceways, and arrange everything so it all FITS TOGETHER like a
well-regulated watch! It has to work LIKE A WATCH!'

The Planter extracted his watch…tapping meaningfully on the dial.

Robert Broughton said nothing, because he was not sure what to say.
The Millwright took the occasion to summarize his conclusions:

'You begin by calculating The Mechanics of Motion, Levers, Belts,
Pulleys, Flywheels, Friction, and so on. Then, as to Hydraulics, you have
to observe the Area of the Millpond, the Impulse of the spouting bod-
ies, the Pressure of Water relative to the Vanes or Buckets of The Wheel,
and Velocity at the Flume. From this you can Calculate the size of the
Mill Stones in Proportion to the Power of the Fall, and estimate the
amount of corn that can be ground…'

The Planter had had just about enough of this!

'Fascinating! Most LEARNED! You are entirely EXPERT in THE-
ORY! and a man of PRACTICAL EXPERIENCE! But what we need to
know is…Is it POSSIBLE to build a Mill? Where? HOW LONG will it
take to build it? How much will it COST to build? How much INCOME
will The Mill bring in?'

'I have prepared a Plan of the Site of Mr. Broughton's Branch. With
the Millpond located here,' and he tapped a spot well above the Creek, 'I
calculate you can impound four acres of water, average depth nine feet.
During droughts the area of the millpond will of course diminish, but
even if there is only one acre of water remaining, you still have enough
flow and head to turn The Mill.'

Carter Jackson and Robert Broughton bent over, minutely observing
every detail of The Millwright's drawings.

'There is sufficient head for a Wheel eighteen feet in diameter, eight arms…branched and well-mortised…fifty-six Buckets, a Shaft twenty-four inches in diameter. This will drive a runner Stone fifty-four inches across. The Mill House for a Wheel of this size should be three stories high.' The Millwright tapped the papers in front of him. 'I show here the revolutions of The Wheel relative to the revolutions of the Stone, with gudgeons, cogwheels, trundles, and gearing. You will need an inclined road so wagons can unload their corn at the top so as to fill the hoppers and feed shafts. You need at least three sets of stones, as they must be re-faced…as they will inevitably be worn smooth.'

The Millwright's words were incomprehensible to Robert Broughton. Even the relatively well-educated Carter Jackson seemed flummoxed. He fidgeted in his chair, and twisted his pince-nez, bending down over the Plan, as though, with a closer look, the terms and numbers would leap into his head.

'And *THE COST*? And *THE INCOME*?'

Profit, Capital, Interest…these were concepts The Planter handled every day. If he could somehow, *anyhow*, bring the conversation back around to MONEY, he would be…at last!…on *firmer footing*.

'I am unable,' said The Millwright, 'To estimate the cost of building A Mill of this type here in Kentucky. But I *have* prepared a Bill of Scantling, including Estimates of masonry. I give Dimensions and Quantities for sills, joists, posts, girders, plates, rafters, beams, and shingles. As for The Water-house, I give Dimensions and Quantities of sills, spur blocks, head blocks, bray trees and bridge trees. For The Wheel, Dimensions and Quantities for shaft, arms, face boards, shrouds, bucket boards…and so on…'

He turned expectantly to The Planter and Broughton. He confronted blank incomprehension. This was normal. Technical jargon justified his Fee.

'Allow me to simplify:'

'Number One. We are in October. If you begin work immediately, you should be able to complete a strong Dam before the end of the year,' he tapped a drawing he had prepared. 'Winter rains will then fill the Millpond.'

'Number Two. If you wish, you can commission me to order three sets of Millstones. I can do this on my way back to Floyd County, as the quarry is only a half-day off my route. You should have the stones delivered to the Site not later than June First. Whoever will be The Miller will also need good stonecutting tools…and the most convenient place to obtain the tools is right at the quarry.'

'Number Three. You will need a sash saw…which I can order from the forge in Floyd County…and files and whetstones to keep the saw in good cutting condition. I can bring these items with me when I return. The saw must be able to move in an up and down motion at one hundred twenty strokes per minute, with a carriage and ratchets to drive the log into the saw teeth, then pull it back. *I know how* to TRANSFORM *rotary* Power of a Wheel into *reciprocating vertical* Motion. *I know how to arrange the Cogs and Gearing.* Cogs and gears require seasoned hickory, heartwood ONLY. See Dimensions and Quantities.'

'Number Four. I observed a grove of large white oak trees at the head of your holler, Mr. Broughton. We will need every one of those trees. I suggest you begin felling them in January, the minute the Dam is completed.'

'Number Five. I assume you gentlemen normally have your corn entirely planted by the end of May. Therefore, I suggest we begin construction the first of June, and aim to be finished by the end of August. That can be done…IF…the oak trees have been felled and snaked down to the Site, and hewed to the Dimensions given here…' The Millwright tapped the papers in front of him…'And you have a four-mule team, and six laborers…with broad axes, hewing hatchets, wedges, adzes, froes, draw-knives, mauls, augers, on Site *at all times.*'

'Number Six. There is considerable blacksmith work at various stages, and I have prepared here a separate paper detailing the Bill of Iron. The most efficient way to handle this is for The Smith to assemble a Forge at the Site.'

With that, The Millwright paused, and turned to Jackson. '*My Fee* to see The Job through to completion and corn milled, is Three Hundred Dollars.'

At this point, The Planter re-gained the floor, but instead of replying to The Millwright, he turned to Robert. 'Well, Mr. Broughton, given your outstanding reputation, I would be able to loan you CASH to buy the millstones and sash saw. I can RENT you my mule team and six of my strongest negras…AT THE USUAL DAILY RATE. I will loan you MONEY for the Smith, and MONEY to pay Mr. Buford Logan's FEE.'

The Planter paused…to see if Broughton was following his train…'I think, taking everything all together, that you will owe me at the end of construction, SIX HUNDRED DOLLARS. I charge TEN PER CENT per year. However, I will not begin charging INTEREST until The Mill is completed. The question for you is…' And here The Planter paused for a considerable time, and manipulated his heavy gold watch in every possible manner…'Do you think there is enough PROFIT in the enterprise for you to be able to PAY me?'

Robert Broughton turned to The Planter, 'Well, sir, I do NOT have your experience in financial matters. I think The Ford here is growing, people need to grind their corn, need sawed timber…Perhaps we can agree on a few Points: people hereabouts are seeking a way to get their corn ground and their timber sawed. 'There is A Need. A grist Mill and a saw Mill will be *used*.'

'I do not have the cash to pay The Millwright's fee, buy the stones, buy the sash saw, pay The Smith for iron work, and rent your mules and niggers. That is why I came to you, Mr. Jackson, to discuss the Proposition.'

'Call me Carter,' said The Planter, 'If I may call you Robert…?

'Well, Carter, I own the Branch and the Oak trees. It's hard to put a price on that, but the water is essential…that and the timber. Don't you reckon that adds up…to at least half of it…just going in…?'

'Robert, you are AMAZING! Keen intelligence! *Perspicacious*! One-half is PRECISELY the amount I propose!…'

'…What would you say to giving me a Paper…If you do not repay the LOAN within, say, ten years, then I OWN HALF? In other words, A Loan SECURED…by The MILL!'

'And Robert…' here The Planter employed his Virginia-Gentleman charm, which he had in great abundance, and was generous in dispensing…'Robert…There is one more thing, and I DO NOT think you will find it A BURDEN…In fact, you might find it a VERY great help! Homer Sturgill and my daughter Nancy have been married fifteen years now. THE GOOD LORD has blessed them with four fine children. The oldest boy, MY GRANDSON, Carter Sturgill, is fourteen. He is a worker, strong, intelligent, and WILLING. I am disappointed to say this…and I hope that he may some day alter his inclination…but right now, he says he has no notion to be A Planter…even though he would of course inherit much…when God CALLS ME.'

'I think he would make a most WORTHY Miller's Apprentice! Would you KINDLY *consider* that? THIS OLD PLANTER FROM VIR-GINIA…' and Jackson fumbled at his pince-nez, and his voice grew wavery…a Millpond of Sentiment…This Old Planter would take it as *a great KINDNESS and FAVOR!*'

And thus they 'Reasoned Together.'

Paperwork was signed a few days before Christmas 1822. The Mill was completed in August, and was grinding corn and ripping logs well before frost in 1823. Constructing the Dam and The Mill was the hardest labor Robert had ever undertaken. He felled forty huge white oaks, and as many chestnuts and poplars. It took Carter Jackson's ox team and slaves eight days to snake the heavy logs from the head of The Branch to the site of The Mill, near where it empties into Marrowbone

Creek, and another six days to skid thirty loads of stone down The Branch to the site of the Dam. And that was *The Beginning*!

In addition to his Water, his Timber, and his Labor, Robert assumed the biggest financial Risk of his life...with absolutely NO clear idea if...or when...or whether...he would EVER be able to repay The Debt. *The Planter held all the cards, and of course took No Risk at all! He never did...*

Year by year more came...and squatted. Like hopeful young settlers before them, the newcomers also sought a better life. When there was no more bottomland up Marrowbone Creek or over the north ridge toward Red Bird, they grubbed corn up the steepest slopes. After the game was shot out, they relied on cows, sheep, and thin razorback hogs. Corn patches grew larger. By the time Hargis and Maggie's grandchildren were grown, the land was useless for hunting, as the forest held little game. It was useless for timber as the giant trees, and many small ones, were gone, hastening the relentless erosion. The land had been gutted and, as soil accumulated over millennia washed down hillsides to be deposited on floodplains miles away, it was stripped of its hide. Farms were less productive, families reduced to bare subsistence. Cabins went unrepaired; some fell off their foundations; roofs leaked. Clearings became trash-filled hog-wallows, privies overflowing into springs and creeks. People themselves seemed to erode, children dying of croup, men and women dying young of vague fevers. All were inexorably diminished. Poverty led to bitter fatalism. No one intended it; most were simply unaware: New Eden had been milked dry, hollowed out, and a listless apathy descended. Barrels of raw whiskey were the main source of money, and the proximate cause of a malady afflicting many.

THE SAWYER
H.C. BROUGHTON, 1849–1935

◆ ————————————

James Broughton's cabin still stands on Red Bird River in Clay County, just over the Bell County line. It is where he raised his family and where, in 1845, he died. He is buried on a hill overlooking the cabin…the cabin where his son Gilley 'Black' Broughton was born in 1818, the same cabin where Gilley's son, also named James after his grandfather, was born; and where his grandson, Henry Clay Broughton, was born in 1849.

In 1869, Henry Clay (H.C.) Broughton, dressed in heavy brogan shoes, home-knit wool yarn socks, a hickory shirt, and homespun jeans and coat, rode over the ridge, down Marrowbone Creek, and across The Ford. He felt *rich*, because in his pocket was $51 earned from 'coon and possum hides he had trapped and tanned. He was on his way to pay court on a tall lovely girl he had met at a three-day Camp Meeting. He slept in a nearby barn, but spent every day that summer at The Garrett Farm. He was five feet six inches in height, Wanda Garrett, five feet eleven. H.C. had piercing blue eyes, an unkempt mustache which seemed imposingly large on a very YOUNG man, and the beginnings of a small belly. The differences in height stirred doubt, but The Garrett Family finally realized the couple was bound and determined. H.C.

Broughton and Wanda Garrett were married…a family-only affair…in 1870 in The Jackson-Sturgill Chapel near Wasioto.

H.C. never attended school, but by combining his native intelligence with patient coaching from his wife, was, within a year of their marriage, able to read a little, though he never read for pleasure. He kept his accounts in his head, and he never made a mistake on what was owed to him, or what he owed others. For the first five years, Wanda handled all of the paperwork for his business transactions. But by the time he was twenty-five, H.C. was supremely confident of his abilities…*and with good reason*. He never again involved his wife in business matters.

They began married life in a log cabin overlooking The Cumberland River. H.C. cleared land and raised crops to provide for his family, but saw immediately that the real money was in felling and snaking logs. By working from dawn until dark six days a week, he had within a year earned enough to build a proper two-story frame house from timber he himself felled and which was sawed at The Mill, the one started by his Uncle Robert, now operated by Carter Sturgill…No 'kinfolks' here: Sturgill charged his Standard Fee.

H.C. got the best price for giant black walnut trees, but there was simply no way to get them to market except down the Cumberland river. Unfortunately, walnut logs are sinkers and cannot be floated. H.C. got around this by lashing walnut logs to huge poplars…excellent floaters…and which also fetched a good price. He drifted his log rafts forty miles downstream to a sawmill at Williamsburg. He continued to begin his workday just after dawn. But he now had enough cash to hire gangs of men to work beside him…and other gangs, led by Foremen he had carefully selected. He also hired 'water boys' to cool off the teams, throwing buckets of water on the horses and mules…and in summer, on the backs of workmen as well. For eighteen years, H.C. made good money off walnut and poplar trees, felling every big log anywhere that could be snaked down to the river…huge logs suitable for Victorian furniture or Grand Rapids veneer. Much hardwood was exported to Europe.

H.C. worked hard, and he had an exceedingly sharp entrepreneurial eye. He was also extremely frugal, a characteristic most often seen in those who are timid and afraid of risk. H.C., however, was confident, many said over-confident, of his judgment, and was willing to take a chance even when others held back in fear...He would Take A Chance if he had calculated the risks and benefits in his head. He was a devoted exponent of the ancient proverb, Buy Low, Sell High. He operated his business on what he called 'H.C.'s Rule of Ten':

'I will buy ANYTHING...timber, land, wagons and teams...and I'm not even concerned about the PRICE!...PROVIDED I see a very reasonable chance that what I buy will return TEN TIMES what I pay...THIS YEAR!'

In 1888, the Louisville & Nashville extended its rail line from Corbin to Wasioto. Financial insiders, stockholders and friends of The L&N Board, had learned of the railroad's plans, and saw an opportunity. They invested in a steam-powered sawmill, shipped by barge from Pittsburgh and by rail from Louisville. The mill was sited at Wasioto, upriver from The Narrows, where the L&N crossed The Cumberland toward Middlesborough. The inside boys had a sure-fire investment...except for ONE LITTLE THING.

H.C. had been buying standing timber, and options on timber, constantly since 1871. By this time he owned virtually all of the timber for forty miles upstream. He was quite prepared to sell logs to the new sawmill, just as he sold logs to the sawmill in Williamsburg. But he had *cornered the market* on easily accessible timber. He knew it. And his price went up and up.

He owned the raw material. They owned The Mill. Why not work together?

After two decades of backbreaking labor, H.C. had saved enough to buy controlling interest of the mill. The minute he was in charge, he discarded the old-fashioned circular saw, replacing it with a modern band saw, which increased production by a factor of four. In 1890, age 41, he placed a great boom across the Cumberland to hold floating logs as they awaited their fate in *his mill*. The L&N had run a spur right into his Mill, and he could now ship sawn timber, greatly increasing his profit. H.C. had become a major lumber supplier, no more need of mills or Timber Agents. HIS MILL brought in more cash than he imagined possible. He continued buying thousands of acres of standing timber…and then began buying timber LAND, outright.

Exploring geologists had begun to describe vast beds of bituminous coal the wooded hills…and H.C. had heard the reports. Soon, with a view to coal mining, he began buying underground mineral rights as well. Just as he hired gangs of lumberjacks and teams of mules, he similarly hired squads of attorneys. They camped out in County Clerk's offices, searching out dubious titles, lawyering and dickering to obtain rights to timber and minerals. They often acquired mineral rights from illiterate farmers for a dollar an acre, sometimes less, even when it was certain that underneath the land lay millions of tons of coal. Kentucky's infamous Broad Form deed, then and up to 1990, permitted the owner of mineral rights to do anything, *anything whatsoever*, to extract the mineral wealth, without any further permission or any further payment to the landowner. The ignorance and poverty of subsistence farmers made for easy pickin's. Poor hillbilly farmers watched helplessly as their land was ripped and gutted. Lawyers and coal operators made great fortunes.

By 1907, H.C. owned outright, or owned the mineral rights, on 34,000 acres of land containing millions of tons of coal. But he needed railroads to transport his coal to the coke furnaces and steel mills of the industrial North and East. Unfortunately, he could not persuade L&N to extend its rail line to his property, mostly in the northern part of The Cumberland Valley. In exasperation, he built The Wasioto & Black Mountain Railroad himself. It was a daunting challenge…but it was a carefully calculated gamble, not crazy at all. He owned the land, he owned the sawmill, which provided oak for ties and trestles, and he had gangs of workmen thoroughly familiar with mule teams and dynamite. As the owner of a very successful and prosperous timber business, he also had access to Capital…in Louisville and Cincinnati.

The completion of the railroad in 1911 opened the rich coalfields of Harlan County. When L&N bought his line in 1915, H.C. received an enormous new infusion of cash. As the L&N snaked its rail lines up the rivers and creeks of The Cumberland Plateau, H.C. raced ahead, buying more land and more mineral rights. He was now a big time coal operator, opening scores of mining camps in Bell, Harlan and neighboring Counties.

Mining camps sprang to life almost overnight, bearing names like Henry, Wanda, Clay, and Black Dinah [after dynamite]. He extended his railroad up Marrowbone Creek, and opened the Gilley and Hargis coal mines there.

By 1917 he owned 57,000 acres. Buying coal land and leasing it was more profitable, and much less bother. Real estate became his chief business. He was elected a Bell County Judge, and in old age enjoyed rocking on the porch of his white-columned Victorian Mansion…atop The Old Indian Burial Mound at Cumberland Ford…with a fine view up Marrowbone Creek toward Red Bird…toward the old cabin of his grandfather, James.

In 1931, he gave the State two thousand acres on Pine Mountain, west of The Narrows, which became the nucleus of Pine Mountain State Resort Park; the CCC [Civilian Conservation Corps] built roads, trails, and cabins for overnight visitors. Giving the land away was a good business decision, as H.C. thereby escaped taxes.

Blight had killed all the chestnuts, there were no coal deposits on that side of Pine Mountain, and he and his timber crews had already felled the most valuable trees; the virgin forests had been cherry-picked, leaving behind stumps and waste. The timber boom left nothing of lasting benefit for the mountains or for Kentucky: no furniture industry, no tradition of craftsmanship. Forest preservation and management began only AFTER severe damage was done.

Henry Clay Broughton died in 1935, age 87.

H.C. would not recognize parts of Cumberland Valley today. Much of his coal land has been contour mined, and gigantic draglines have removed entire mountaintops, choking creeks and valleys with debris, creating acidic runoff that killed crawdad, fish, and every kind of natural aquatic life [though bass are returning to The Cumberland River]. Some surface-mined land has been 'restored.' But even on so-called reclaimed land, H.C. would be unable to trap enough animals to make any money at all off hides.

More than two centuries of ruthless exploitation has been particularly hard on the people, most descendents of early settlers. They are strong; they have survived, and they will. But in the process, Kentucky's human resources, like all other resources of the region, have been largely stripped.

Game animals, at least in areas close to settlements, were quickly shot out in the 18th century [though some game has been re-introduced].

Virgin topsoil was washed down hillsides by logging and bad farming practices [though conservation farming is slowly taking hold].

Irreplaceable forest giants were sold for a pittance, 1880-1930. This denuded the hills; with little vegetation to absorb the rainfall, sheets of water run unchecked down the hills, and floods devastated downstream villages and towns [though today some are protected by expensive berms and dikes]. Trees re-grow, but it will take many centuries to recreate even an approximation of the primeval forest encountered by early settlers. Many visitors are entirely unaware that Great Smoky Mountain National Park was, in 1930, the scene of vast environmental devastation. The road to Cades Cove, for example, follows the route of a logging railroad that hauled out millions of board feet of prime timber.

Coal mining has hollowed out mountains and, what is more sad, hollowed out miners and their families. [Coal also provided jobs, but at a great cost in injuries and diseases like emphysema and 'black lung'.]

The issues are complex. But many in southeastern Kentucky, like their kin elsewhere in Appalachia, seem empty, devoid of hope, withered husks of their proud and fiercely independent ancestors. Is it an exaggeration to say that good, brave people were systematically '*hollowed out*'? Young people leave as soon as they realize there is no work and few opportunities; young people have been Kentucky's principal export for generations. 'Rip, rape and run,' and 'Get it all NOW!' never asks…What Is the CONSEQUENCE?…and, Is It Worth It? Even sadder is that much of the devastation was abetted by the mountain people THEMSELVES! They are intensely attached to 'the hills and hollers of home,' tied by kinship, sentiment and strong emotion. At the same time, they have been complicit in the destruction of the hills and hollers.

No valuable black walnut trees remain.

W.C. would find…*no valuable trees at all.*

[See *Our Southern Highlanders*, Horace Kephart, U. of Tenn. Press, 1913, 1922; *Tumult on the* Mountains, Roy B. Clarkson, McClain Printing Co., Parsons, WV, 1964; *Miners, Millhands, and Mountaineers*, Ronald D. Eller, U. of Tenn. Press, 1982; *Eastern Old-Growth Forests*, Mary Byrd Davis, Ed., Island Press, 1996; *The Appalachian Forest*, Chris Bolgiano, Stackpole, 1998]

PINEVILLE, KENTUCKY
CUMBERLAND FORD, 1750–

◆

Dr. Thomas Walker's youngest child, Peachy (b. 1767) married Joshua Fry II (1760-1839), grandson of Walker's good friend, Colonel Joshua Fry, also of Albemarle County, Virginia. Joshua Fry II was a member of the Virginia legislature before moving to Danville, Kentucky. Among their children was Martha Fry; she married David Bell (d. 1847), and among their children was Joshua Fry Bell (1811-1870). He graduated from Centre College, studied law at Transylvania University in Lexington, and practiced law in Danville. He served (1845-47) in the U.S. House of Representatives. During service in the Kentucky House of Representatives (1863-67), he was responsible for the creation in 1867 of the 112th county, named for him as Josh Bell County. The name was changed to Bell County in 1872.

Many houses I knew as a boy are long gone. But many remain, not affected by the destruction occasioned by the building of a giant earthen dyke to spare the town from repeated flooding.

Pineville does not at present have a Wilderness Road marker in or near the town, and nothing to call attention to a geological wonder, The Narrows. There is no sign at all denoting The Ford, which gave the little town its first, historic name. The Cumberland River was the last physical barrier to the overland settlement of Kentucky. The Ford was thus part of the overland gateway to what Virginians called 'The West,' not less important than Cumberland Gap. Today, the Ford is virtually inaccessible, obscured and buried under the great dyke of 'The By-Pass.' This could be easily corrected: U.S. 25-E and the floodwall impede access to The Ford from the southern bank of the river. But a sign could direct visitors across the Pine Street Bridge, where The Ford can be seen clearly from the site of the former bread factory of The Modern Bakery. Visitors will not know the significance of The Ford, however, unless there is an explanatory marker.

Dr. Walker notes in the *Journal* of his 1750 exploration, that he found coal in Bell County, and brought back samples, perhaps to prove to The Loyal Company that there was something of economic worth on the western side of the Blue Ridge. The mountains all around Pineville are, or were, black-veined with seams of bituminous coal. But despite a cornucopia of mineral *wealth*, what is left is endemic *poverty*. Most mining jobs are gone; most families in Bell County today survive on remittances: Black Lung payments, disability payments, Social Security, WIC (Women, Infants and Children) payments, Food Stamps.

Rapid industrialization after the Civil War created an insatiable demand for coking coal to make steel. The vast coalfields of eastern Kentucky were known, but How To Get It? How To Get It Out? Eastern industrialists hired sharp lawyers to buy up the mineral rights. The lawyers were often good ol' boys with familiar surnames, the few who had managed to get an education…many only one generation removed from the poor families they were trying to bilk.

Railroad commodores did the rest. In a few decades they snaked steel up every valley of the Plateau. A creek holler with one lone cabin could become, in a few weeks, a booming coal town. Frame tenant houses were thrown up quickly, pump-wells for water, outhouses for 'sanitation.' Coal operators got rich. Many, or their prosperous descendants, are now happily retired on horse farms near Lexington. Lawyers and doctors also made out well.

But the uneducated men who went deep inside the mountains, who blasted seams and shoveled till they dropped, were often killed or injured by blasts that went awry, pockets of methane, rock falls, electrocution. Old miners survive on government remittances. Many are dying from coal dust they inhaled decades ago. Their old age is a time of distress. They cough constantly, gasping for breath, as 'black lung' kills them...very slowly, but very surely.

The coal life held great appeal for subsistence farmers in remote hills. Coal brought electricity, hospitals, motion pictures, and stores. Poor ignorant farmers came eagerly, not that the poor ever have much choice: families have to eat, and you simply cannot make a living farming eroded hillsides. In boom years, miners had good salaries and hope. But wage jobs in the mines weakened proud mountain traditions. Some companies controlled towns like little kingdoms. Miners were expected to vote as the company wanted; miners paid high prices at company-owned stores, a policy often enforced by paying the miners in 'scrip' which could buy food ONLY at the company store; they were treated by doctors paid by the company; they lived where they were told; they were *expected to be silent.*

The story of coal in eastern Kentucky, or anywhere in Appalachia, is a tangled skein of investments, boom-and-bust economics, jobs, emotional and bitter labor conflicts and violence, and grief from accidents. Coal has affected the quality of life of thousands. The tentacles of the industry run deep into the lives of families, and coal permeates every aspect of Kentucky politics.

Pineville prospered in tandem with coal; it provided services to perhaps forty coal camps all over Bell County. The town reached its peak population, a little under four thousand, during World War II; coal was in demand, still produced in underground mines and requiring lots of workmen.

Today, coal employs a mere fraction of those who worked underground. Giant earthmovers shave off entire mountaintops. Two or three

men operating enormous machines, plus a handful of drivers maneu-
vering behemoth Mack trucks, can now produce the same amount of
coal that formerly required a small army of miners.

The town served both the operators, and the miners and their families. As the Seat of Bell County, you went to the County Court Clerk's
office to file deeds and mortgages, obtain marriage licenses, file birth
and death certificates. Pineville was where you settled lawsuits, pro-
bated wills; it was where the murder trials, and there were plenty, were
conducted. Lawyers had offices all around Courthouse Square.

The most colorful of the lawyers was Walter B. Smith, who every year,
astride his palomino horse and wearing a Kentucky Colonel's white
fedora and black string tie, led the parade which opened the Mountain
Laurel Festival. Another regular in the parade was 'Johnny Bull,' a semi-
hermit eking out an existence in a cave on the Mountain, who marched
along wearing a coonskin cap, attired in nondescript hunter's rags, carrying his rifle. He was certainly 'a character,' but he looked more like a
bum than a Long Hunter.

July The Fourth was celebrated with fireworks (sometimes a kid's
finger blasted off), and a parade, whose biggest contingent was veterans
of World War I, all in American Legion caps; they fired rifle volleys 'in
memory of fallen comrades.' The first Fourth of July parade I remember
included a few veterans of the Spanish-American War, marching slowly.
Leading the parade were four grizzled survivors of The Civil War,
pushed in wheel chairs. I have no idea on which side they fought. Both
The Ford and Cumberland Gap were chokepoints for troops from both
the North and the South during The Civil War, and Breastwork Hill,
which overlooks the Ford, was carved with long deep trenches.

Pineville businesses included insurance companies, accounts, surveyors, mining engineers, and two banks, The First State Bank was run
by George Reese, whose policy on loans seemed to depend not on written statements or collateral, but on word-of-mouth reputation and his
opinion of the character of the applicant. He boasted that his bank

never closed during the worst of The Depression. (His house had the town's only tennis court. It seemed a conspicuous display of wealth. I didn't own a racket and had no idea of the game, though I was allowed to roller-skate on its concrete surface a few times.) There was also The Bell National Bank, which did fail during The Depression.

Hardware stores such as Brandenburg & Gibson, and Smith-Cawood, and others, stocked carbide and carbide lamps, coal oil for kerosene lanterns, iron kettles, tools, and barrels of nails; some had sections for specialized mining equipment; all stocked heavy axes and mauls, and chains and come-alongs for snaking logs. There were several feed and grain stores; they also sold vegetable seeds and just-hatched chicks, which, incredibly, survived a two-day trip by parcel post from hatcheries in central Kentucky.

The Delaware Powder Company sold dynamite, blasting caps and fuses. The Kentucky Utilities office did engineering in its Pineville office, dispatching crews to string lines all over the County, as did Southern Bell Telephone. There was a lumberyard and a gravel-and-cement works linked to a quarry; their biggest customers were the State highway crews, at work more or less continuously paving and improving roads to the mining camps. There were carpenters, plumbers, electricians, and house painters. The L&N employed several score men who lived in town: engine drivers, firemen, brakemen, switchmen, conductors, telegraph men, ticket-sellers, track maintenance workers, and repairmen. There was a bottling plant, which produced grape- and orange-flavored soft drinks (though Coca-Cola and RC Cola came by truck from Middlesboro). The Modern Bakery produced bread as soft as cotton, and small cakes, perfect for a miner's lunch pail, of equal parts sugar, flour, and lard, with enough artificial flavor and artificial color to make it attractive; their trucks delivered to all the mining camp company stores.

There were three dealers in new automobiles and trucks, and a dozen gas stations and repair shops. The latter was where I went to get a patch hot-glued to fix a hole in the inner tube of my bike tire. There were a half-dozen physicians, four dentists, a couple of chiropractors, and a hospital (the latter constantly expanding). Health care still provides reliable jobs, and hospitals and nursing homes are among the few thriving institutions in Southeastern Kentucky's coal counties, which have endured many years of economic boom-and-bust.

Four funeral homes and a cemetery served those medicine failed to save. There were three motion-picture theatres, The Gaines, The Reda, and, later, The Bell, built on a vacant lot which had been used up to 1938 for traveling Medicine Man shows, complete with Indians. Saturday was the big day for the movies; us kids loved serials and cowboy shoot-'em-ups, especially those with Red Ryder, Hoot Gibson, and Hop-Along Cassidy. We were also suckers for the silly 'Buck Rogers' antics of Buster Crabbe. For a while during The Depression, the Gaines held weekly drawings for chinaware. The restaurants were all run by Greeks: George Karloftis, the Sideris family [Koula, Athena and my Cub-pack buddy, Tony] at The New York Café, the Counides family at The Olympia Restaurant, the Regas family at the pool hall which featured Cincinnati 'Five-Way' spaghetti, with chili, cheese, onions, oyster crackers, and beans.

I had childish contempt for those of my cohort who spent their nickels on pinball machines; shoving a machine this way or that struck me as stupid, nothing more than brute force. But pool took *skill*! I really loved that pool hall and flattered myself that I was beginning to know how to handle a stick so as to 'spot' the cue ball and set it up for the next shot. Today, in my, how shall I put it? 'mature' years, I sometimes say 'I got my education in pool halls and libraries.' An exaggeration, but not entirely off the mark.

There were also 'dives' like The Terminal Lunch, Coffee Pot Lunch, the Hole-In-Wall, and a few so notorious they had no sign whatever out front…not to mention 'Dime Street,' which got its name from the going rate charged by the pathetic whores, mainly 'colored,' in their miserable 'cribs.'

The clothing stores were run by Jews…Lazarus Scott, Abe Euster, Harry Isaacs…families down from Cincinnati, selling cloth and needles and thread, shoes, some ready-made clothing. On my way back from The Depot I often passed an old man, perhaps the scion of one of the families mentioned above, reading *Forward* [*Forwerts* in Yiddish]; the Hebrew type struck me as the most utterly foreign thing I had ever seen. J.J. Newberry 5-and-10 Cent Store sold notions, the cheapest possible candy, and Big Little Books. Four drug stores, FloCoe, Gragg's, Bingham's and Morgan's, had marble soda fountains dispensing lots of 'Co-Cola.' I was often penniless, and the 'soda jerk' would sometimes amuse me by offering me a 'pine float,' a glass of fizzy water with a toothpick floating on top. In addition to prescriptions, the drug stores carried an amazing variety of patent nostrums. Pineville also had a dress shop, a gift shop, a flower shop, two barbershops, and a shoe repairman. A watch repairman was kept busy working on railroad watches, his bench up against the glass store-front, so passers-by, often kids like me, could see him at work, a loupe screwed into his eye socket, as he adjusted a complex mechanism with incredibly tiny tools.

The town was on the route of itinerant Gypsies, and every summer brought a small-time circus and a ratty carnival. For me, the main attraction of the latter was the Ferris wheel. The circus and carnival set up in a big field in Wallsend, no more than three blocks from our house, when we lived there. In the early 1930s, we also had a few barnstorming pilots, in their open-cockpit biplanes. They landed in Martin Green's pasture at Four Mile, and took thrill-seeking townsfolk as passengers for $5 per half-hour ride!

The Post Office was a central meeting-place, and it's not surprising that Paul Greene, who was 'at the window' day-in day-out for forty years, wrote, decades after he retired, detailed reminiscences of his friends and patrons. There was also a Western Union office, and three bus stations, Trailways, Greyhound, and a rinky-dink company that ran buses up the coal hollers. The Continental Hotel was where the drummers, dealing wholesale to local merchants, spent the night before catching trains back to Cincinnati. And there were six churches.

Pineville sits in a cup, whose handle begins at The Narrows, where the river slices a dramatic gorge through Pine Mountain (a water Gap, not a dry pass, and not a 'saddle' like Cumberland Gap). This is where U.S. 115 turns northeast toward a string of coal camps along the way to Harlan and beyond. Just south of the 115 turn-off is the entrance to Pine Mountain State Resort Park and the Laurel Cove Amphitheater. [Today, the Park boasts a 19-hole mountain golf course, 'Wasioto Winds,' new and VERY gorgeous.] In the 1930s the Park had just a few log cabins, but construction began in 1935 on The Lodge, which has been constantly expanded and improved every decade since. A stone building offers spectacular views of the ravines and deep woods on the southwestern side of Pine Mountain.

'Old Pineville' began at The Narrows and continued as a row of houses along the river to The Ford. The modern town was laid out after 1880 on the floodplain. Pine Mountain and Chained Rock are at the town's back, and it faces the Cumberland Plateau, full of the game and timber sought by Long Hunters and sawyers, and beyond that, the Blue Grass and rich farmlands sought by pioneer settlers. Straight Creek drains the north side of Pine Mountain, and the Cumberland River drains the southern side of the Mountain. Perhaps a hundred creeks run into the Cumberland. The river is called 'Poor Fork' until it gets to Harlan, where Martin's Fork from Cumberland Mountain joins it, as well as Clover Fork, which drains water from Big Black Mountain.

Creek names provided identification and provenance for individuals and families. We knew who hailed from Beans Fork, from Brownie's Creek or Little Clear Creek, and we knew who came from Log Mountain or Laurel Hill. Like small towns everywhere, and most especially small Southern towns, everybody knew everybody else. There was an easy familiarity. 'Hi,' 'How ya' doin?' 'Haven't seen you lately; been away?' We knew everybody instantly by sight. And not only did everybody in town know you, they knew ALL ABOUT YOU. They knew 'Yore Mama,' they knew 'Yore Daddy,' they knew 'Yore kinfolk' stretching back at least two generations. There were no secrets in a little Appalachian town. There was No Place To Hide.

Things grew more animated on Saturdays, usually a day off for the mines. Miners and their wives and children would come to town…in the 1930s on mule or horseback, in wagons, or by train. In the 1940s, they came more often by truck or bus. Miners were easy to identify; the men had coal dust in the creases of their face and hands, and a characteristic distant stare, 'plumb wore-out.' The center of the action was Courthouse Square. The miners all used tobacco, some cigarettes, others corncob pipes; some dipped snuff, and many of their wives did too. Those who chewed tobacco seemed to have a contest going, as to who could spit the farthest. The discarded gobs of tobacco were truly disgusting. The sidewalks around the Square were stained brown, and it took a long spell of rain to wash them clean.

The miners and their families had a rhythm to their Saturday-in-town. The kids would pretty much run loose, or go to the movies. The women-folk would shop for yard goods, thread, needles, store-bought clothing, or essentials like lard, corn meal, baking powder, flour, salt, sugar. They patronized Kroger, and the A&P, sometimes the I.G.A. store. Many town folks preferred J.L. Saunder's U-Tote-Em, which despite its name, would actually DELIVER.

The coal miners mostly hung out, whittling, chewing, spitting. Quite a few shopped for hundred-pound-bags of sugar and ten-gallon cans of malt extract, basic ingredients for distilling 'beer' into 'singlings.' The mash was then run back through the still again, 'doubling,' until the liquid from the coil produced a characteristic 'bead,' indicating fifty percent alcohol, 100 proof corn whisky, commonly known as 'white lightning,' though 'pop skull' is a more accurate description of its effect.

It was of course dispensed in half-gallon and quart Mason or Ball fruit jars, which had by this time replaced earthenware jugs. But the mash had to be cooked in copper and distilled in copper; if not, the stuff would poison you. Bad liquor apparently damaged the central nervous system, and we saw a few guys limping around town with what was called 'Jake Leg,' proof that if you were going to drink, you had best have A Reliable Bootlegger.

For those of us who lived in Pineville, the most popular entertainment was people watching. Most of the miners were transplants from subsistence farms, many from very remote hollers. Those of us who lived in town certainly had, and still have, a distinctive Kentucky 'twang' to our speech. But our 'twang' was as *nothing* compared to the peculiar idiom and strange words used by the miners, especially those not long removed from the hollers. I cannot reproduce their speech, and you will have to search out very OLD 'Bluegrass' recordings to hear even an approximation of it. [If you are interested in this, Cratis D. Williams' book, *Southern Mountain Speech*, Berea College Press, 1992, is a good place to start; Joseph Sargent Hall made a number of tape recordings of the speech of old timers in the Great Smoky Mountain area.]

We also enjoyed the many street musicians, both black and white, picking and singing, a tin cup strapped to their guitars. Some were truly desperate, down *hard* in the depths of the Depression. Some played and sang well; others had more spirit than skill. Another great entertainment was mountain preachers, many totally illiterate. But they all had a spell-binding way of 'testifying'…usually non-stop, the rant punctuated here and there by a raw gasp to suck in air, then more gesticulating and thumping of the Bible, turning pages most of them could not read. Once in awhile the preachers would include snake-handlers, who, confident in their faith, would reach into a burlap 'croker sack' and pull out a handful of rattlers or copperheads.

The most dramatic entertainment, sometimes truly dangerous to be near, was the fights, mostly with fists, sometimes with knives, and sometimes with guns. Louise once exited J.J. Newberry's five-and-dime, when a bullet, fired from a pistol a block away on the other side of Courthouse Square, banged a hole into the brick just above her head.

DECEMBER 1, 1943–
SEPTEMBER 4, 1946

◆

I ran away from home on December 1, 1943, my fifteenth birthday. Old stuff for me, as I had run away at nine, walking forty miles up the Harlan road toward what my childish brain imagined as paradise at Aunt Rachel's. Maybe it wasn't paradise, but it was at least an escape from the chaos and crises caused by my father's drunken binges. I simply could not take any more of his hung-over blubbering promises to take the pledge, which of course never 'took,' nor any more of my Mother's tears and histrionics, and what I thought was her stupid credulous hope that maybe…THIS TIME!, maybe…he will stay sober.

I ran away again when I was eleven, walking to Barbourville so nobody in Pineville would see me leave. I wandered aimlessly around the town. As night fell, I realized I had no money, no food, no place to sleep, no plan, and no possibilities. I hitchhiked back to Pineville late the same day.

My hegira at thirteen was more serious, more planned. I started out with more cash from my paper route, and a fierce determination to find a job, any job. Just GET AWAY! I walked to Barbourville, and caught the bus from there to Cincinnati. When I got there I had absolutely NO IDEA what I would do.

It was night when the bus pulled in. Like some light-dazed moth, I headed for the bright neon, and soon was in the middle of the honky-tonk area, a rough place of bars and bums. I realized I had no business there. I was scared and heartsick. Within an hour a policeman stopped me.

'Whatcha doin' here boy? This ain't no place for kids. What's your name? Where you from?'

A quick ride in a squad car, and I was dumped off at the Juvenile Detention Center. There were bars on the windows. We were watched like a hawk by tough guys with guns, marched to the showers, marched in to eat. It was indeed a jail…for kids…most of them mean as hell, and they scared me to death. I was miserable, I felt very sorry for myself, and I was worried I was going to hell…fast! I had no idea what was going to happen to me.

After three days of wild apprehension, Aunt Rachel showed up to claim me, and we drove back to Pineville. It was a long trip, plenty of time for hours! of non-stop tongue-lashing, with many stern moral lectures.

'Louise is a good woman. She works her fingers to the bone for you and Dick. She worries herself sick about you! Don't you have any sympathy for your Mother? Why would you do this to her? Go ahead and cry! I don't care if you cry! You *ought* to cry and you ought to be mighty *ashamed* of yourself. You've got brains. But brains won't do you one bit of good if you don't use them! I just don't know what IN THE WORLD we're goin' to do with you!'

When we got back to Pineville, tears were shed by all, abetted by much melodrama and hysteria. My personal melodrama was learned behavior, I feel sure now, taught by Louise herself; she was A MASTER of self-dramatization.

What really got to me was THE SHAME! Everybody in our little town would KNOW! Know that I had run away, Know that I had been in jail, Know that I had been dragged back, Know that I had 'betrayed' my Mother, a Good Woman who Worked Herself to Death for Her Kids. These thoughts drove me just about out of my mind, and I very seriously threatened to jump out the second-story window of our apartment in the I.L. Hopkins building. Louise sent word to a neighbor, and Dr. Wilson showed up. He gave me an injection of something, and I was soon asleep.

But shame lingered. '*They*' had caught me **this** time. '*They*' had brought me back. But *I would leave again*. I HAD to! I was certain I MUST get away!

After Judge was fired and left town in 1941, Louise had no income; nonetheless, Judge's many creditors hounded her nonstop. Uncle Jim paid off the Railway Express embezzlement, and Rachel and Bill often paid our rent and helped out with food. But Louise was sick with worry, and *worry was what she did best*. In fact, worry occupied most of her time and energy.

She looked everywhere for work, but the only job she could find was wrapping cakes at The Modern Bakery, paid twenty cents an hour. She had to stand nine hours a day, pushing the gooey pastries over a hot-plate, which sealed the cellophane.

We were living hand to mouth. It was obvious that Louise was really not able to take care of Dick and me, which is why in 1941 she sent me off to live with Ralph and Anne, and in 1942 sent me off to Red Bird Settlement School. When I got back to Pineville, I began to deliver *The Courier-Journal*; I washed dishes in The Continental Hotel; I built early morning fires for an old woman who lived alone on Cherry Street, and I brought in coal and chopped kindling for her; I hoed corn for twenty-five cents a day…anything, anything at all, to bring in a little money.

Louise let me keep what I earned. I was a growing teenager and always hungry [adults claimed we ate so much because we had 'a hollow leg']. With a little pocket change, I was able to supplement the food at home with grilled cheese sandwiches and malted milkshakes at the soda fountains. Shelby Thompson, the obese pharmacist at Bingham's, who claimed we were related though my grandmother Haley Garrett, would enquire, 'Do ye want an' egg in that?' I always said 'Yes!'

My mind was racing. I began to rationalize: not only would *I* be better off if I left Pineville as soon as I possibly could; but I soothed my conscience by reasoning that my leaving would be a great favor to my Mother; one less mouth to feed, one less body to clothe. If I were out on my own, I would be doing Louise and Dick *a BIG favor!* I secretly saved my paper money, and began to plan. And on my fifteenth birthday, I made my move.

After it got dark, I crept across the Passenger Terminal Bridge, and climbed about halfway up Pine Mountain, looming up above the L&N tracks. It was December and I had no warm clothes, since I was headed South and 'trav'lin' light.' I tried to sleep, but my teeth chattered all night, I shivered uncontrollably, my bones shaking with cold. I imagined I might freeze to death right there on the hard rocks of Pine Mountain. I looked down as the lights in our little town slowly went out. I felt very sorry for myself. Was this what I wanted? No! But I HAD to get away!

The next morning, I walked to Middlesboro and caught the train to Chattanooga. I *thought* I had A Plan, but in fact I had *nothing*…just a vague notion. I thought that if I headed south, at least I might be warmer. I thought I might go as far as Florida, maybe pick oranges. I'd find a job, any job. I'd find a place to sleep, anywhere, an empty carton, an abandoned house.

Others had done it, and I had read about them. Why couldn't I make it, too? My non-stop reading had filled my teenage brain with dreamy romance. I read all of Richard Halliburton, all of Mark Twain, all the Horatio Alger I could find. Dale Carnegie's bestseller consisted mainly of thumbnail biographies of wealthy and successful people who had Started With Nothing and were now Captains of Industry. There were also stories like these every month in *The Readers Digest*. I also drank deeply from book-jacket blurbs about famous writers, and was naïve

enough to believe what I read. THEY had made it on Luck and Pluck. I
COULD TOO!

I slept the first few nights in the railroad station in Chattanooga,
though the policemen in the Terminal had an extremely EFFECTIVE
way of discouraging bums and drifters: they simply WHACKED a billy
club across the insole of anybody sleeping on the benches. Searing pain
shot up your legs and spine, and in a single instant, you were WIDE
AWAKE!

I didn't much care for that. So with what money I had left, I caught
the train to Atlanta. I can't remember how, but I somehow stumbled
onto a job boxing shoes in a factory. I moved two weeks later to a similar job in the shipping department of the big Sears & Roebuck warehouse there. I ate in restaurants, usually opting for a stack of pancakes,
which filled me up and could be had for twenty-five cents. If I was going
to be 'a hobo,' I thought I ought to dress the part. So with my first wages
from boxing shoes and Sears orders, I bought a pair of bib overalls, a
cheap flannel shirt, and some 'work boots' (which, in the middle of the
war, were not made of leather, but of heavy canvas).

Most nights I slept in the USO downtown. There were and are lots of
Army bases around Atlanta, and the USO offered cots in the basement
where soldiers could sleep until they caught the early-morning bus back
to their base. I found an unlocked door, sneaked inside, and was sound
asleep before anybody knew whether I was a solider or not.

But one night the USO basement door was **locked**!

I usually walked the four or five miles from the Sears warehouse to
downtown Atlanta, and by the time I got to the USO, I was so exhausted
I was just about out on my feet. I stumbled along, and came to a hotel.
Surely, I thought, there must be SOME quiet corner in this building
where a teenage hobo might get a little rest. I sneaked in and climbed
the backstairs to the fourth floor. I went up and down the hallway, trying every door to see if one might be unlocked. Sure enough, I found an
open door, and behind it a room with a Big Double Bed. But *wait!*

Suppose the hotel had policemen or security guys, just *looking* for bums sneaking into their rooms? What could I do? If they saw me, I would surely be arrested, and spend more time in another Juvenile Detention Center and be hauled back home in shame. So I crawled under the bed, and was sound asleep by the time my head hit the floor.

I don't know what time it was when I awoke, but it might have been two in the morning. The springs of the bed were bouncing up and down in that ancient procreative rhythm. I think I must have yawned or coughed. Anyway, the man heard me, and I saw his head leaning down over the side of the bed.

'What the SAM HELL! What are you *doing* here boy? Get out of this room right now!' Thank God he didn't hit me or call the cops.

With the USO door locked, and hotels not a possibility, I began to think it was time to get out of Atlanta. So I headed south again.

In Macon, I saw a sign in a restaurant window, 'DISHWASHER WANTED.' I went in and talked as polite as I knew how to the Greek owner. He agreed to let me sleep on the floor of the kitchen, and would provide meals, which I also had to eat in the kitchen. And he would pay me ten dollars a week. That job had several things I liked...namely food and a place to rest! I would have stayed awhile, if it weren't for the fact that the detergent in the dishwashing machine was eating the skin off my hands, which were also continuously bleeding from cuts caused by broken glassware.

I lasted three weeks. When I left, the owner gave me an extra ten. I was rich! So, like every softheaded American adolescent with more hormones than judgment, I caught the bus for New York City. Isn't New York where the writers are? Isn't that where you find *bright lights*...and glamour? I knew all about it: I had seen the movies!

The Manhattan bus station was next door to the YMCA. I stayed at the Y about a week, foraying out for long walks all over mid-town. When I got as far as Union Square, I knew I had reached Mecca and my *hajj* was completed: The Academy of Music had vaudeville and movies;

there was the *PM* newspaper; cranks and crazies were ranting non-stop in the Square! Joy! Best of all, there were three full blocks of second-hand bookstores! I loved it!

I got a job at a delicatessen, delivering pastrami, liverwurst, and garlic pickles to brownstone apartment buildings around Gramercy Park, a Park that, incidentally, was locked; the only private 'Park' I had ever heard of.

About a hundred yards from the bookstores, at the corner of Tenth and Broadway, was Grace Episcopal Church. A sign out front said 'Youth Shelter.' Sounded good to me. I was certainly a 'youth' and boy! did I ever need 'shelter'! They took me in, no questions asked...at least for the first week or so.

After two months on the road, my adolescent brain imagined I had Landed On My Feet. I had a job, I had books, I had a place to stay. I felt I was at last really 'on my own'!

Then one day, the Counselor in charge of the place asked softly, very low-key...'Don't you imagine your Mother might be *worried* about you?' I allowed as how she was, indeed, a World-Class Worrier. 'Why not just write her and let her know that at least you are *ALIVE?*'

He saw my letter, and using her name and address, telephoned her. I don't blame him. That is precisely what he should have done. I realized later that I had been thoughtless, willful, selfish...thinking only of myself, apparently not caring one damn bit about the Mother who loved me and was 'sick with worry' that I might be dead, or worse. [And WORSE might well have happened. I was VERY *lucky*...then, and later.]

When she got The Call, the Counselor reported that my Mom was melodramatic and tearful, standard operating procedure for her. Only this time, perhaps after talking with the Counselor, she took another course. She realized that bringing me back...for the fourth time!...to a little town in the Cumberland Mountains would simply *not work*. She had to find *another way*.

She got in touch with the widow of her cousin Allen Cooke [aka 'The Human Cork']. Ada Dozier Cooke was born in Wallins Creek, and though she had perhaps only a sixth-grade education, was blessed with more energy and determination than anyone I have ever met since. She was a simply UNSTOPPABLE force! She had come to Washington with her two daughters, Martha and Mildred, for the simple, logical reason that there were plenty of jobs in the wartime Capitol. She was right; there were.

With intelligence and energy, she had no sooner arrived in Washington than she arranged to call on 'her' Kentucky politicians. She struck up a friendly acquaintance with Flo Bratten, a redhead from Somerset, who was 'Secretary' [in fact, she ran everything in his office] to Alben Barkley, Majority Leader of the Senate. Somehow, Ada managed to persuade Mrs. Bratten to help me.

I was not there, and Ada never told me what she said, but I imagine lots of drama and tears. 'This boy just wants a normal life; he wants an education. He can be *SAVED*! You can DO it, Flo. *SAVE* him! Give him the chance in life he needs.'

Flo Bratten was convinced, somehow, that I was indeed salvageable. Within a week I was under Senator Barkley's patronage and enrolled in Capitol Hill Page School. The Architect of the Capitol began to pay me the FABULOUS! salary of $1,800 a year. Ada told my Mother that I would be a Page Boy. But their duties struck me as stupid and demeaning; I preferred evening hours as an elevator operator [I was pretty sure the night shift would leave me plenty of time to READ!] in the Senate Office Building. Flo Bratten also arranged THAT.

I bunked up with Ada and her daughters the first week, then moved to a boarding house on East Capitol Street, within walking distance of The Senate.

There were giants in the Senate in those days...Walter George and Richard Russell of Georgia, Arthur Vendenberg of Michigan, Lister Hill of Alabama, Carter Glass of Virginia, and Hiram Johnson of California, who had been there since World War I. Almost every senator seemed to me extraordinarily vivid and larger-than-life. My recollection of these personalities makes today's politicians seem anemic and tentative by comparison. But I was too naïve, too green, to understand much of what was going on, and I suspect that may be why the very young continue to be hired…they're no threat to *any*body.

The marble halls, the mahogany-paneled offices, the gilded caucus rooms were overwhelming, yet even a hillbilly Holden Caulfield soon learned to make distinctions. Harry Truman was friendly and industrious; Robert Taft had the heaviest briefcase and put in the longest days.

But it was hard to take some of them seriously. Glen Taylor of Idaho went from 'Singing Cowboy' to Senator, and, after he lost office, to purveyor of toupees. Clyde Hoey of North Carolina, with his wing collar and frock coat, seemed to be in costume, and, like the Deacon in the comic strip 'Pogo,' spoke in Gothic script. 'Wild Bill' Langer of North Dakota never lit his cigars, but chewed them at both ends with the cellophane wrappers still on. The brass spittoons found in all the halls and offices were truly needed. Theodore Bilbo of Mississippi wore the same hand-painted silk tie every day, the violent colors muted by the gravy and grease of years of barbecues and fried-chicken dinners. Tom Connally of Texas exuded the charisma of a Senator…a **Roman** senator. With white hair flowing down to his shoulders, a black suit, string bow tie, and an imposing girth, he could have been sent over from Central Casting…but he was sharp and effective.

I soon learned them all by sight. Some would look right through you…they could ignore you and make you FEEL it. Others were simply tired, or distracted from talking to an almost-constant entourage. There were a few, however, who noticed 'a new boy' and were willing to stop for a moment and chat. Those I recall most fondly are perhaps forgotten today. James Tunnell of Delaware was unfailingly kind. Henrik Shipstead of Minnesota became a kind of father figure for me. George Aiken of Vermont was a thorough gentleman, as was Theodore Green of

Rhode Island, a tiny patrician elder with pince-nez glasses and Victorian courtesies. I greatly admired tall, craggy Leverett Saltonstall of Massachusetts…his demeanor, his strange accent.

I appreciated the pecans from Georgia, the citrus from Florida, and other home-State largess, which Senators or staff would sometimes share with the kid on the elevator. I had plenty of ties to go with my regulation white shirt and dark trousers, thanks to James Mead of New York, who seemed to have a bottomless supply of 'Billingsley Bows'…freebies from the owner of The Stork Club.

On the night shift, I saw the occasional floozy and smelled telltale odors from Senators and staffers who would regularly stagger out after 'committee work' with the bottle. On several occasions, filibusters or war crises caused late-night sessions. It was exhausting, but it was exciting.

Everything should have been perfect, but the lack of adult supervision got me into trouble. I was on my own all right…no rules, and no one to enforce them had there been any.

Page School sounded wonderful, but in 1944 it consisted of six airless rooms in the Capitol basement and a bare minimum of courses. Classes began at 6:00 in the morning, and ended at 11 a.m., in time for the pages to deliver documents required for that day's session. For a teenage sleepyhead like me, getting to school at the crack of dawn, or well *BEFORE* dawn!, was just about impossible…with no one to rouse me out of bed and push me to class. My attendance became increasingly erratic, and I finally stopped going altogether.

The principal informed Mrs. Bratten, and she called me in for a little talk. I told her things would be okay if I could just attend regular public school. Barkley had to find a job for a kid from Paducah, so she arranged to transfer me to the patronage of Sheridan Downey of California, a holdover from the Townsend 'Share the Wealth' Plan ['Thirty Dollars Every Thursday'], who also had a slot on the night shift. In September I enrolled at Eastern High School, but dropped out, yet again, after only a month. I then registered at Western High School, where I lasted about two months. The nice thing about the public schools was they didn't report you to the Senator's office. I began tenth grade four times (five, counting Pineville). But I never finished even the first semester.

For almost three years I fell between the cracks. To the people in Senator Downey's office I was simply a name for whom they provided patronage as a courtesy to the Majority Leader. Once I left Page School, there was no supervision at all.

I didn't plan it, but I somehow managed to create my own 'School Without Walls.' English instruction was handled by The Public Library [I always left with as many books as I could possibly carry] and by Paul Pearlman, who ran an absolutely sensational secondhand bookshop near 17th and G streets. Pearlman was a genius; he inspired you to read.

History was absorbed from the Magna Carta and Constitution in the Rotunda, and from Statuary Hall and the Brumidi frescoes which decorated walls all over the Capitol. Current events class met every day, enlivened by the excitement of radio equipment and the flash of the Speed Graphics at hearings and press conferences.

I learned a little physics in experiments with speed and momentum on the subway car that ran between the Capitol and the Senate Office Building, and I conducted some unauthorized acceleration tests with the elevators [I called myself a 'Vertical Engineer' or 'Indoor Aviator.'] Chemistry consisted of experimentation with ethyl alcohol. Geography was gleaned by exploring the rabbit warren of corridors and secret passages in the basement of the Capitol, and by asking visiting constituents: 'Where you all from?'

Culture was not ignored. In the Beaux-Arts Capitol Theater at F and 14th streets, I had music instruction from an excellent orchestra led by Sam Jack Kaufman (who, decades later, inducted me into the American Federation of Musicians), not to mention seeing 'a major motion picture' and six vaudeville acts...tumblers, contortionists, dog-and-pony acts, The Harmonicats, tap dancers, xylophonists, seals blowing horns, sometimes a famous band or a famous singer: the sort of thing we later saw on The Ed Sullivan Show.

There was also a pipe-organ sing-along, as we followed the bouncing ball. It was awesome: the house lights would go down, and a powerful spotlight lit the edge of the orchestra pit. An enormous gilded console slowly rose out of the darkness, lifted by hydraulics to the level of the orchestra seats.

Sex education took place at The Gayety Burlesque, under the inspired tutelage of Hinda Wausau. Sex was of course the lure, but I really enjoyed the split-second timing of the blackout farces, the stupid antics of the comics, and the pit band.

Once a week I had recess at the Glen Echo Amusement Park, which also had good Swing bands in The Spanish Ballroom. Physical education consisted of swimming and basketball at the YMCA; on two occasions I fell hard against the basketball floor, splitting open first my left, then my right eyebrows; you can see the scars today. The other sport I tried, for the two months I was at Western High School, was track and field; I have no idea how I got into that particular event, but the race I ran was the 400-yard 'dash,' essentially the 100-yard dash, run *four times with no rest. I vomited after every race.*

My school refectory was the Senate staff dining room, where all meals featured 'Senate bean soup'…manna for a kid from Kentucky. If I were on my way to my night shift from my copy boy stint at *The Star*, but running late and no time for a restaurant, I'd pick up a half-gallon of buttermilk from High's Dairy Store. Sometimes I mixed it up, a quart of buttermilk AND a quart of butter brickle ice cream; no adult to tell me, 'eat your broccoli.'

My fellow elevator operator, Grant Kirkham, a student at the Georgetown University Dental School, ably provided health advice and dental treatment. Grant persuaded me that I absolutely HAD to get my teeth fixed, and of course he was right, but the process was so painful it could fairly be called TORTURE! The School used old-fashioned pulley-operated drills, and no Novocain except for extractions [of which I had two]. He later used me as a guinea pig to demonstrate his skills so as to pass the Maryland Dental Exams. You can still see the gold foil fillings he jackhammered in on that occasion.

I studied singing with a guy who had a little 'studio' on the second floor, up over the stuffed polar bear on G Street in front of Zlotnik the Furrier. With him on piano, I made a recording on the primitive Wilcox-Gay, which cut grooves into waxed cardboard; I still have the record. The song is a 1934 Harry Warren standard, 'I Only Have Eyes For You.' I also sang, 1944-46, as often they'd let me, with combos at several USO's.

While still in Pineville, I had been a regular at our high school hang out, Brookings Confectionary. It had a Wurlitzer jukebox with bubbles of air rising up the lighted tubes on left and right. The jukebox played all the latest hits by Swing bands and crooners. I hung out…waited, watched, hoped, dreamed, longing to join the 'In Crowd.' But I was *pimply and nerdy*, never a cool combination. I never once had a date, and was so bashful and naïve, I doubt I would have known what to do, if I HAD ever had a date with, as the song says, 'A Real Live Girl.'

This was the era of Big Bands, and if you wanted to be popular or even ACCEPTED, you had to know how to dance. I had never held a girl in my arms, had never learned to dance. But this seemed to be correctable, so I spent some of my money for classes at Arthur Murray's…and got to do both. Later, when I was older and in an Air Force uniform, some of the girls said I was 'a good dancer.' WOW!

It was a bizarre academic program, and I ended up without a piece of paper. But for me, pig-headed and stupid as only an adolescent can be, formal school seemed out of the question, and no one on Capitol Hill was hassling me. Time soon began to hang heavy on my hands. Working the elevators at night left my days entirely free. There was only so much reading and roaming I could do.

So I went to what was then Washington's dominant newspaper, and ended up with a job as copy boy, and later photographer's apprentice, at *The Evening Star*. I hoped I might learn to write just by **proximity** and osmosis. My role model was Jack Bell, who covered the Senate for the Associated Press, and who sometimes took the time to reveal How He Got That Story.

Two facts I observed immediately: most of the reporters were two-finger typists, which seemed strange then and, strangely, persist even today. The other thing was far more **important**. 'Writer's Block,' or moony dreaming in front of a blank piece of paper, would get you Fired Out Of There…Fast! The Re-Write guys, for example, sat at typewriters with headphones on their ears, typing fast, taking down info dictated by a reporter, perhaps at The Scene of a Crime. Depending on the time of day and when the next edition 'closed,' The Rewrite Man had maybe five, ten, minutes to understand the 'Facts,' arrange them in a logical sequence, and then, typing as fast as he could, write a story that had a beginning, a middle, an end…and sometimes a little poetry to boot. These guys were PROS; I admired them A LOT. I also admired 'The Slot Men' who kept track of all the assignments, the pace of The Rewrite Men, edited all the copy, monitored deadlines, scanned the AP and UP news tickers [my job was to tear off the copy every five or ten minutes and rush it to them], and who decided where stories would appear in the paper.

I enjoyed 'running copy' from reporters to Editors; the latter were 'the gate-keepers'; they decided what would, and would NOT, be printed. I relished trips to 'The Morgue,' a repository of virtually all of Washington's history since The Star had begun in the mid-1800's. Another job was running out to fetch coffee and doughnuts. I also had to distribute the other papers, *New York Times, Washington Times-Herald, Washington Daily News*, and so on. No way to AVOID keeping up with Current Events.

The photography part, which came a year later, was interesting, though I had to DO IT RIGHT. I entered the pitch-black darkroom, no red 'safety' light, in fact NO light. Then, by feel alone, I opened the Speed Graphic slide-holders, opened the box of sheet film, slid in the film, making sure the emulsion side faced the correct way, then closed the slide. I loaded film into perhaps thirty or forty slides every day.

I also developed the film. The photographers would come back from a shoot, and toss me the exposed slides. My job was a to 'soup 'em up' and do it *correctly*…right chemicals, right amount of time, right wash bath, and so on. I also made prints, and copied some photos, mainly when people brought in photos of loved ones who had died, and *The Star* copied the photo so we could run a picture with the obit.

My most common assignment was to carry the camera bag for the photographers. It contained the heavy, bulky 4x5 Speed Graphic, a flashgun, perhaps twenty flash bulbs, an equal number of slide holders, and a heavy tripod. This was nothing but grunt work. Most of the assignments were humdrum, a photo of such-and-such a church for the weekly 'Neighborhood Page.'

The only really exciting job was carrying the bag for photographers who were 'covering' a morning news conference at The White House. I was never once allowed inside The Oval Office, not even allowed close. But when FDR's news conference was over, sometimes even before, the photographer would rush out, throw me three or four slides, and tell me to RUSH! back to *The Star*. There was a motorcycle with a sidecar waiting just outside The White House fence. I leaped into the sidecar and we made it to *The Star* in less than two minutes.

I RAN up the stairs, elevators too slow and uncertain, ran into the darkroom, and 'souped' the film in a special 'dynamite' developer we mixed for just that purpose. I made a print while the negative was still wet, and then RAN down to the Stereotype Room, where they turned the print into a piece of lead with BenDay dots, suitable for the print-ing-press. We usually managed to get the photo into the First Edition, which 'closed,' as I remember, about 11:00 a.m., normal for an after-noon paper [few of them left in 2002]. Excitement like this really turned me on to newspaper work, and made me even more determined to somehow Learn To Write!

Up to this time, my only experience with photographs was with quarter-in-the-slot booths, which produced no more than an image, and a crummy one at that. At *The Star* I started to develop a serious interest in photography. I bought a Kodak Retina, which had a fine lens and a pretty fast shutter. Best of all, it could be folded so small I could carry it in my pocket. Aside from The Minox, used by spies, this was one of the smallest cameras, and a good one. I took lots of photos with it. Ancient Retinas are today a collector's item.

Lunch was always hit-or-miss. Sometimes I'd go to The Waffle Shop, across the street from the old Earle theatre, just down from The Capitol Theatre. Or I'd go to the Planters nut shop across from Woodward and Lothrop department store on F Street, and buy as many cashews as I could afford, always broken ones, which sold for half price. I also ate often in the Vita 'Health Food' lunch counter next door. I just loved the weird concoctions they produced, carrots and other veggies whirled in a Waring blender until they turned liquid and could be drunk; or soy-beans in various combinations. This was the era of Gayelord Hauser, and people were starting to be more interested in such things. I sampled all of it.

I have no idea why I never once set foot inside any of Washington's fabulous museums, not the spectacular Mellon Art Gallery, nor any of the great history museums. **Nothing**. I guess people watching on F Street, Washington's main shopping drag, was simply more exciting. Maybe working two jobs, and checking every single bookstore, took up so much time, there was simply no more room in the day.

I LOVED *The Star* and continued to work the two jobs until August 1946. *The Star* was owned by the Kaufman and Noyes families, and they had a fine staff. I greatly admired editorial cartoonist Cliff Berryman, who first drew the bear cub and associated it with President Theodore Roosevelt, dubbing it 'The Teddy Bear'; he also affected a turn-of-the-century ARTIST look, white hair down to his shoulders, and a HUGE 'Windsor' floppy bowtie. His son Jim took over as cartoonist after Cliff retired, and Gib Crockett moved over from the Sports after him. I was so in awe of editorial writer Lincoln Gould that I was scared just to enter his office; I think I tiptoed around him. Reporter Miriam Ottenberg and the sports writers served as my school psychologists and career counselors. I recall a crash course in linguistics and etymology when A Rewrite Man helped me decipher the Latin scatology [sometimes when his text was especially rough, Rabelais would switch to Greek!] in a Modern Library edition of *Gargantua* and *Pantagruel*, which Pearlman judged suitable fare for a naïve and timid 16-year-old.

I bought every Modern Library title I could acquire at a cheap price. I didn't care how dog-eared the binding, I wanted THE TEXT! I also tried to read as many titles as possible from Mortimer Adler's list of Great Books: The King James Bible, Emerson, Thoreau, Hawthorne, Edgar Allen Poe, Fennimore Cooper, Melville, Robert Frost, the plays of Eugene O'Neill and Thornton Wilder, Faulkner, Hemingway, DosPassos, Steinbeck. I loved *The New Yorker's* 'Mr. Arbuthnot, The Cliché Expert,' the work of E.B. White and S.J. Perelman, and the highly stylized backward sentences of *Time*. I loved O. Henry, and thought the essays in *LIFE* magazine were a model of the form. I tried a few Shakespeare plays, and made it through a few; I loved his Sonnets, and, being a moony teen-age romantic, of course had to see if I couldn't write a few myself. I slogged through as much Plato, and as many Greek and Latin playwrights and historians, as I could handle, though, I am sure, with only childish comprehension.

Living conditions were almost as haphazard as my education. Wartime Washington was crowded almost to bursting, and housing was VERY scarce. Mealtime at the boarding house became 'The Battle of the

Platters,' and if you weren't aggressive about reaching and grabbing, there would be no food left! My sleeping room was a converted closet.

The other roomers on my floor were three twenty-year-old girls who worked as typists at The Navy Yard. This was pre-TV, so we talked a lot every night, and they sort of adopted me. The three of them concluded they could find a better place to live than a boarding house, so they moved out to a two-bedroom apartment in Mt. Rainier. One reached this Maryland suburb via streetcar; in downtown Washington the cars got electricity from underground rails, connected to a 'shoe' which ran through a slot between the tracks; after the line crossed Florida Avenue, there was a change-over: the underground shoe was disconnected, and a pole was unhooked so the car got its electricity from an overhead wire.

When the third girl, Gertrude Winarski, returned to her job at the Kotex factory in Menasha, Wisconsin, the remaining two really HAD to find a third person to share expenses. They asked me if I was interested, and I moved in, a separate bedroom, heaven after my closet at the boarding house.

It was innocent enough, but hardly what one would have chosen for a young man my age. I recall an occasion when Jean Price Artrip [who, incidentally, weighed over two hundred pounds] invited some members of the basketball team from her hometown, Waynesboro, Virginia, to bunk up at our apartment following a game with Alexandria. The boys broke training, you might say, with several fifths of booze and stayed up all night playing poker, with the record player blaring. The police arrived about 3 a.m. The boys were in their shorts, and the girls, who'd been vainly trying to sleep so they could get to work the next day, came to the door in their nightgowns. The cop took a long, slow look: 'I don't care what you kids do in here, but for God's sake, keep it quiet!'

The girls were not always kind, though I suppose they weren't any harder on me than older sisters have always been toward kid brothers. I remember they showed me some pages of 'literary' pornography they had typed up while at work. I had never read anything like it! I was sixteen, pimply, hormones raging…You can imagine what happened! My pajamas began to bulge with a strange but utterly predictable swelling; the girls thought this was the funniest thing in the world, and I think they tried the trick on me another time, and I fell for it again.

Once, while the girls cooked up a Thanksgiving dinner, I went off to an afternoon movie, one of the 'Topper' series. Perhaps you don't recall them; I scarcely do myself. The films were shot in high key, mainly tones of white…and exuded an Art Deco atmosphere of ultra-sophistica-tion…lubricated of course by enormous shakers of martinis. This seemed to me great stuff: so THIS is what it means to be an adult! Topper himself seemed a genuinely *happy* old roué. Maybe the secret was his constant intake of *gin.*

In any event, back from the film, and sitting down to dinner, the girls suggested we all have some 'drinks.' After 'Topper', that sounded like a splendid idea, and we filled our glasses. They seemed able to handle their quota, but this was, so far as I can recall, the first alcohol ever to hit my brain. It administered a total knockout. I discovered I could NOT manage to get the fork to my mouth, and when I misjudged, the tines nearly put my eye out. I eventually passed out, head down in the pota-toes and gravy. And so it began.

The two girls and I once decided we ought to spend a summer Sunday on a little picnic in the countryside. So we went down to Union Station and caught the train to Rockville, about fifteen miles north of the Capitol. Rockville was an old country town with only a general store; it was surrounded by dairy farms, orchards, rolling countryside. We were way out in the country all right! Today, of course, it is one con-tinuous strip mall, one of the ugliest in the United States.

Because of the teasing and many other reasons, I thought I would be better off on my own. I leaped at the chance when I saw an ad for a fur-nished room at 1736 F Street. The rooming house was located behind the YMCA and right around the corner from Paul Pearlman's Bookstore.

It was also close enough that I could walk to *The Star*, though I had to ride the streetcar to my Senate Office Building job.

The War had ended with two atomic bombs, and there were many articles in newspapers and magazines about what would become of us now that we were in The Atomic Age, with everyone everywhere at constant risk of radiation and death. Newspapers printed maps showing how much of New York and Washington would be obliterated if and when, and they implied it was only a matter of time, *The Big One* hit us. I was very worried.

I thought quite seriously about what one could do to escape death by blast and fire and radiation. I reasoned you had to get out of the Northern Hemisphere, because winds would spread dust carrying deathly radiation everywhere. Secondly, you also had to get as far away from any likely target as you possibly could. I consulted a globe in Brentano's bookstore, a wonderful shop [I wish it were still there!] on F Street right next to The Capitol Theatre, and determined that New Zealand was THE safest place. It was well below the equator and far from any industrial sites likely to be targets. I wrote their Embassy asking what I had to do to emigrate; I thought I might actually do it. But the more I learned about New Zealand, its isolation, and, especially, its sheep, the less enthusiastic I became.

There had to be another way.

So I joined The United World Federalists. We had just survived a bloody God-awful World War. But already The Soviet Menace was beginning to be talked about. Maybe it was just a matter of time until we were in the middle of another one. UWF made a lot of sense to me...and I was as active as I could manage to be. I started a correspondence with Cord Meyer, whose extraordinary career took him from decorated solider who lost his left eye battling for Guam, to liberal activist, to manager of covert operations for the C.I.A. from 1951 until 1977 [including subsidies to American student groups and a literary magazine, *Encounter*, through which, though I was unaware of it ('no need to know'), I 'touched' him, once removed, yet again]. Interesting that Meyer became an important official of the Central Intelligence Agency, and I spent nearly three decades as an overseas propagandist, also doing my bit in The Cold War…which I now think of as World War III. World War IV began September 9, 2001.

As teenage idealist, I knew Meyer in 1946 mainly as a founding member of the United World Federalists, where he fought for controls on atomic weapons. He had also been a special assistant to Harold E. Stassen, a member of the U.S. delegation to the 1945 conference that founded the United Nations. I was also reading all the articles I could find by Norman Thomas, Robert Hutchins, Norman Cousins, and other non-Communist pacifists. I renewed my interest in UWF in the fall of 1949 at Princeton, and remember marching behind Nassau Hall banging a bass drum in a parade, which included John Kemeny and Albert Einstein, both at The Institute for Advanced Studies. Kemeny, a brilliant mathematician, largely invented the BASIC programming language and was later President of Dartmouth.

UWF had just one little problem: not a single country in the world was willing to give up sovereign independence to any kind of World Government. The more you thought about it, the more obvious this became. And if there was no 'One World,' there was no means of ever preventing another War. I finally concluded that UWF was a dream…a logical dream, perhaps…but nonetheless a dream. We would have to find some other way to live together on this globe and not kill each other.

The Moment of Truth came for me in September 1946. For two and a half years Capitol Hill patronage had employed me…and ignored me. I had lived Wild and Free. But I was now almost 18…with three full years of high school yet to finish. I went back to Western High School and asked if I could be re-admitted.

The principal, Mr. Danowski, gave it to me straight: 'Looks to me like you're washed-up. You have *squandered every opportunity* you have been given, and you have been given plenty. I doubt you'll EVER amount to anything. I'm *sorry* for you. You have dropped out of Western twice. We don't WANT you here any more! Good-bye, and good luck! You will *need* the luck.'

That was the first time in perhaps three years that an adult had given me straight truth. I needed that, BAD, and was it ever a wake-up call!

It was fall, there was a soft rain falling, and as I walked away from Western High School for the last time…a school that DID NOT WANT ME!…tears were streaming down my cheeks. *I was certain my life was OVER!*

SEPTEMBER 4, 1946–
AUGUST 31, 1949

◆

Two weeks later I was in an Air Force uniform. Even a teenage nitwit as self-absorbed as I was, could understand I NEEDED structure and discipline. Maybe the military would teach me something useful. Best of all, The War was over; nobody was shooting at anybody, thank God!; and by enlisting when I did, I would receive the *full benefits of The G.I. Bill.*

You can't beat that!

I was 'processed' at Fort Meade, outside Washington. I had some crazy idea that I might be able to escape my three-year obligation, if I ever decided I wanted to escape: all I had to do was not raise my hand and not repeat 'the oath.' (I was much taken then, for reasons that now escape me, on not 'swearing' to ANYthing!) A veteran Master Sergeant later set me straight. 'Don't matter a hill o' beans whether you raised your hand or WHAT you said. You signed The Contract, 'affirming' you're 'In for Three.' And that, my friend, you ARE!'

We 'inductees' were then sent on a nonstop troop train to Lackland Air Force Base in Texas. While I was asleep I had my foot burned by some delinquents who thought it good fun to give somebody a 'hot foot.' The Base was located outside San Antonio, and was used for Air Force basic training, which I survived. I actually liked the marching and the cadence songs. I fired 'grease gun' machine guns, Colt 45s, and M-14 carbines, earning a Sharpshooter Medal on the latter. We were also exposed to tear gas, apparently just to make sure we knew that the stuff really would control a crowd, and that you'd darn well better put on your mask, if gas is released.

A secondary job was with Special Services; my co-worker in this was Spanky McFarland, who had been a chubby child star in the Hal Roach 'Our Gang' and 'Little Rascals' films. He was a conceited pill, and a goof-off.

I was then sent to Scott Air Force Base in Illinois, near St. Louis, to be trained as a cryptographer. I thought this was an absolutely terrific job assignment. I had always enjoyed fooling around with words. Best of all, they would teach me how to TYPE…fast and accurate. I loved typing: I knew that if was ever going to make it as A Writer, I'd have to be GOOD and FAST.

The machines we were trained to operate six decades ago are now antiques. I enjoy looking at them in the Smithsonian's Museum of American History. The one we used most was called 'SigAba,' and was based on the Nazi Enigma machine. We started our workday by adjusting the rotors for that day's 'setting.' The SigAba was thought to produce an unbreakable code. We also used a small 'field' machine, the M-209. This little device, about the size of a toaster, would fit on your knee. You needed a special notched screwdriver to adjust the pins and ratchets, to set it up for that particular day. The third encryption tool we used was simple paper and pencil, the so-called 'One Time Pad.' These Pads were still in use fifteen years later when I was in the Foreign Service in Bamako, Mali in West Africa. Whatever the machine or method, they all produced five letter 'groups,' gibberish like this: *xzfgp qplmn ssois qzxnm*…and so on.

I am NOT giving away any secrets here, as these machines are so ancient they are openly sold; you can buy them on The Web at e-Bay. Nowadays, with powerful computers, and software you can download free off The Net, you can encrypt text into a code so powerful it is probably, indeed, absolutely unbreakable.

Next stop was Argentia, on the southeast coast of Newfoundland, a former fishing village…windy, cold, raw. Not much to say except that it convinced me I really did not want to live in Newfoundland. Maybe in summer it might look a bit like Maine!

Then, my longest assignment, at Lages Air Force Base, on the island of Terceira in The Azores; called 'Terceira' because it was the third of the Azores islands to be discovered by Columbus.

From Terceira, I managed to bum a few rides on planes going this way and that. I flew over to the island of Santa Maria, interesting because this was where the Pan Am 'Clipper' planes stopped to refuel. From 1935 to 1941 the big flying boats hop-scotched across the Atlantic, from Miami, to Bermuda, to Santa Maria, to Lisbon. A café at Santa Maria also introduced me to periwinkles and other exotic seafood, washed down with gallons of *vinho verde*, the light white wine of Portugal, similar to 'May Wine' of Austria. The men of the Azores have long had a reputation as skillful and brave fishermen. They also hunted whales, and 19th century American whalers hired many. Half the families I met in the Azores had a relative of some kind in 'Nova Bedford,' Massachusetts.

An 'R and R' [rest and rehabilitation] trip took me to Ponta Delgado, biggest city on the biggest island in the chain, Sao Miguel. I met the U.S. Consul there, Clifton Wharton, at that time one of the very few Negroes in the U.S. Foreign Service. After I myself was in the Foreign Service, I met his son, Clifton, Jr.; he had followed his dad into that career. My destination on 'the big island' was a luxurious resort hotel, 'Terra Nostra,' high up in the mountains, with stunning manicured gardens with every kind of semi-tropical plant. The village was called 'Furnas' because of its bubbling steam vents, heated by the volcanoes that had formed the island chain.

I was at this juncture well into my 'I *WILL* be A Writer' mode, and the dangerous percolating mud-pits seemed an exotic locale that I could perhaps use. So I tried my hand at a 'formula' detective story, trying to copy the stylized plots of this specialized genre. I produced a cocka-mamie mish-mash involving a devilish creature that appeared out of the steam, and who disposed of his victims by hurling them into sulfu-ric vent holes. I duly submitted my effort, but it was course 'rejected,' a turndown with which I became quite familiar over the years. [HINT: if you can't take rejection, do not, repeat NOT, attempt a career as a Writer or as a Musician!]

The hotel oozed luxury and Old World charm, and I made the most of it. My first morning, I ordered 'breakfast in bed,' not because I really WANTED breakfast in bed, but because that is what I had seen rich people order in the ritzy hotels which were the fantasy backdrop of Hollywood musicals.

The real attraction for me, though, was The Casino, which had roulette wheels. But I had no money I could afford to lose, and had never pushed any coins into the slot machines at the Officers and NCO Clubs. But the Casino did have a fairly classy quintet, strings, piano, and drums, playing mainly tangos. Well, Arthur Murray had *taught* me how to dance a tango, and I had lots of fun with the ladies, most of them of 'a certain age,' at The Casino.

I later bummed a ride on a plane going to Lisbon. I walked all over the hills and mosaic plazas of the city, determined to see every single thing of interest. Sometime after nightfall, tired, I found myself in front of an attractive and sophisticated-looking nightclub. Quite lovely dance music produced by a large orchestra was wafting out the enticing door-way. Naturally, I went in.

Strange place: a half-dozen men, most of them with attractive dance partners, and LOTS of pretty senhoritas, maybe thirty of them, seated alone at tables around three sides of the room. Having learned all those tricky dance steps at Arthur Murray's, this seemed like a golden opportunity, so I used my best Portuguese, and asked a girl to dance. She jumped to her feet and locked her arms around me like a wrestler. She made me think I was her Prince Charming, the guy she had LONG waited for. It took me a couple of bottles of expensive bad champagne to wise up. This joint was an up-scale whorehouse, and EVERY SINGLE GIRL was a hooker! The Portuguese have *A STANDARD*, simple and clear: a girl *is* A Virgin, or she *is* A Whore. That's IT! Nothing in between.

Well, that's one way to get introduced to EUROPE!

I saw a bit more of 'Europe' in Casablanca, where French *colons* were evident everywhere. But I got another shock. I wanted to see EVERY-THING, and had been walking all day non-stop. Well, in the fullness of time, it happened that I simply HAD to use the bathroom. Hooray! What luck! Right there, smack in the middle of the biggest square in the middle of the city, was a public 'facility,' with *TWO entrances*...one clearly labeled *hommes* and the other *dames*. Well, you don't need much French to know which door to enter, so I went through the door marked *hommes*. But I was not quite prepared...

There at the bottom of the stairs, the *hommes* and the *dames* all mingled together, buying tiny scraps of toilet paper from an ancient crone. Male and female nonchalantly entered first one or another of the W.C. cubicles.

Well, Toto, I guess we're not in Kansas [or Kentucky!] anymore...

The island of Terceira was pretty much in the center of the North Atlantic, and when ocean storms hit, there was nothing on our little island to stop them. I remember many occasions when I had to lean into the wind and push HARD! to make it up the hill from the barracks to the Quonset huts of AACS [Air and Airways Communications Service].

Lages is also where I learned to cuss, as Norman Mailer accurately transcribed in *The Naked and the Dead*...fug you, fug this, the word used in every permutation and combination...noun, adjective, verb, adverb. It was a bad habit to acquire, and I hope I've weaned myself from this. Ex-military will understand.

I tried hard to learn Portuguese, and succeeded somewhat; at least I managed to communicate, which few other Americans on the Base ever did. I made friends with some guys in the Portuguese Air Force [it was *their* base; the U.S. just had use of the facilities].

The Portuguese had an unusual way of bull 'fighting.' They 'rented' a bull for the day, tied a thick rope around one of his legs, and then 'fought' in the streets, seeing how close they could get to the bull's horns without being gored. Big heavy fellows on the other end of the rope prevented serious injury. But when the bull charged, we all scrambled up the rock walls lining the narrow streets. These were sharp volcanic rocks; perhaps you escaped being gored, but your hands were pretty well cut up.

Two towns on the island appealed to us guys in uniform. One had a sandy beach, called in Portuguese a '*praia*.' Because this was where the people of the Azores had stoutly resisted an invasion from, I think, the Spaniards, it had been awarded an honorific name, 'Praia da Victoria.' The biggest town was, similarly, not just 'Angra,' but 'Angra do Heroismo.'

The major event on Terceira while I was there was the arrival of the 'peregrinating' statue of 'Nossa Senhora do Fatima,' which recalled the 1917 vision of two peasant girls in the town of Fatima. There was NO DOUBT in the minds of the peasant-farmers of the Azores that this statue could cure disease and assist in other miracles. When the plane bearing the statue touched down, every farmer on the island, and his wife and their children, had assembled. The crowd numbered fifty thousand, all the men dressed in black suit, white shirt, no tie, no shoes. They also carried a black furled umbrella. Their wives were similarly attired all in black, no shoes. It was impressive and memorable.

The most interesting 'cultural exchange' was when a Portuguese sergeant invited me to his home to meet his wife and children, and share a meal. Turned out he had an attractive teen-age daughter. *Hmm!* She ate with us, but said not a word. A few days later I learned that there was a much-admired Portuguese-language film, the life of the great poet Camoes, whose epic, *Os Lusiadas*, describes 'the lights' of campfires in villages on the African and Asian coasts, as his ship sailed from Lisboa along the string of Portuguese forts and colonies strung our like a necklace adorning the continents…Ghana, Mozambique, Goa, as far east as Macau.

The film was being shown at the cinema at the Portuguese base, and I asked the sergeant if he would mind if I invited his daughter to see it with me. 'Of course! My wife and I would be honored!' So, on the appointed day, I arrived at their house, and young Maria and I walked a half-mile or so to the cinema. We never touched. I was startled then, and it's still funny thinking about it: the sergeant, his wife, and their four other children followed us closely, maybe twenty yards back. And when we got to the cinema, Maria and I found seats, while they found seats *directly behind us.* I guess the sergeant and his wife had heard enough about American servicemen to never ONCE let their daughter out of their sight! I think, on reflection, and given *The Standard*, they had it about right.

I played string bass with 'The Masqueraders' (our theme song was a popular hit of the time, 'Midnight Masquerade.') I had little idea what note was where on the bass fingerboard, but I kept time. My main job with the band was singing: my biggie was 'Golden Earrings.' We played three nights a week at The Officer's Club, three nights a week at The NCO Club. Our leader was Ben Wisniewski from Milwaukee, who played a huge button concertina, not my favorite instrument, but Ben could really play it! Our drummer was 'Skull,' who closely resembled his nickname. A pilot flying in and out of the Base played nice trumpet, getting a Clyde McCoy 'Sugar Blues' sound using a glass tumbler as a mute. A few reed players sat in from time to time.

The Reverend in charge of the Base Chapel kindly allowed me to use the piano and Hammond B-3 organ, Standard Issue for military chapels all over the world. I really enjoyed fooling around with the B-3 drawbars and pedals. It inspired me to learn notation and chords, and I began music theory courses via USAFI. I could soon play from lead sheets…melody and chord symbols.

The two Clubs were also where I learned to drink. For reasons that still make no sense to me, the military permitted the Clubs to sell alcohol at twenty-five cents a shot! At those prices, as some of my drunken Air Force friends would say, 'You can't AFFORD to stay sober!' And so it CONTINUED.

I don't know how I managed THIS, since I still stammered fairly often, but I wangled a job as a disc jockey on our little Base radio station, playing jazz and popular music. The records were fourteen-inch acetate discs distributed by the Armed Forces Radio Service. The announcer who led into my little DJ show had heard me sing at the Officers Club and at the NCO Club, and he invariably introduced me with something I'm sure he thought was a real thigh-slapper: 'And now we present Bing Bang Burns and His Bubbling Baritone, brought to you by Bayer's Bitter Bowel Balls, guaranteed to Blast Baloney out of Bloated Bellies without Bursting Buttons.'

For three years, I took scores of college-level course offered by the U.S. Armed Forces Institute. I simply skipped high school stuff and went straight to college-level material, psychology, history, literature, philosophy, the Classics, plays, poetry, music theory. I earned a USAFI high-school 'equivalency' certificate, and also took a battery of college-level proficiency examinations.

And I continued to read. My goal was simple: I had messed up in school, but why couldn't I educate myself? I had no doubt at all that I could it. I read anything and everything. I particularly remember the hundreds of cheaply printed paperbacks, all quality titles, which publishers made available free For the Troops. I grooved on *The Loom of*

Language, and *Mathematics for the Millions*, by Lancelot Hogben. I also read many books by Isaac Asimov, one of the most prolific authors of all time, and by George Gamow. The code room was a perfect place to read and write. We were locked inside a kind of safe, no chance of being disturbed, not with our 'grease gun' automatic weapons and Colt 45s.

Since I had yearnings to be A Writer, I applied for the job of Lajes Correspondent for the weekly newspaper that circulated to all the Air Force Bases in the Atlantic Command. I wrote 600 words every week, mainly who had arrived at the Base, who had left, who was promoted, what the Base was doing. Just then, for example, we were servicing non-stop landings and take-offs as hundreds of C-54 transport planes headed toward Europe and The Berlin Airlift. The newspaper adorned my column with a photo of me. They 'enhanced' the image by painting in stuff over the photo, showing me lolling in a hammock under phony palm trees, my hand holding a glass with a little parasol in it. I was described, accurately I think, as 'The USAFI Kid.' I still have a copy of the issue with my photo-cartoon. I love it!

We didn't have today's computers and word-processors, but we had The Next Best Thing, machines that produced long rolls of punched tape, which could then be fed into Teletype machines. The wonderful part was, the tape allowed you to correct typing mistakes. You could also print out as many copies as you wanted. I have boxes of those old printouts, yellowing Teletype paper, probably decaying into fragments. If I wanted to make the opus you're now reading longer than it is, I might inflict some of that verbiage on you!

AACS was the communications arm of the U.S. Air Force, and had some of the finest short-wave receivers extant. We also had a very huge 'antenna field.' Most nights I scanned the dials, listening to stations in first one language, then another. I managed to understand a word here and there.

The station that really turned me on was Dutch short wave, out of Hilversum in southern Holland. They had a DJ who must certainly be one of the greatest linguists of all time! He had listeners all over the world, and would chat with them, greeting them, introducing the songs, reading their letters...in at least thirty different languages: Dutch, German, English, French, Spanish, Portuguese, Italian, Romanian, Norwegian, Swedish, Danish, Finnish, Hungarian, Chinese, Hindi, Creole, Icelandic, Urdu, Japanese...it went on and on, a simply AMAZ-ING performance, better than a vaudeville show. It may be that he had simply memorized phrases in enough languages to give a convincing impression that he really knew all those tongues. But he sure convinced me! His theme song, which he played at least once an hour, was an English ditty from the 1930's...'A Nice Cup of Tea': 'I like a nice cup of tea in the morning, I like a nice cup of tea with my Tea, and when it's time for bed, there's a lot to be said! for A Nice Cup of Tea!'

No one can know how things might have turned out if I'd had adult supervision, if there had been another kind of living arrangement, or a better school. But today, almost sixty years later, I am certain it is not a good idea for kids of 15, 16, even 17, to run loose in a big city. If Senators and Congressmen continue to hire youngsters, they ought to face up to the turbulence of adolescence and provide some kind of guidance.

By this time, I was 20, had left the Azores, and was now stationed at March Air Force Base not far from Los Angeles. One of my assignments was testing paper from air filters on the roof the code room. We placed the paper in Geiger counters, read the meters, and sent encoded read-ings up 'the chain of command.' We were not told, but we had a pretty clear idea, why we were doing this: we were monitoring fall-out dust, trying to detect from the radioactive signature, whether the Soviets had or had not exploded an atomic bomb. I imagine code rooms in Japan, Hawaii, and Alaska were also monitoring. We later learned that in 1949, the Soviets had indeed exploded an atomic bomb, thanks in part to American communists, who supplied them with data from Los Alamos.

A few years later both countries had the even more awesome Hydrogen Bomb.

The Base was about forty miles from Los Angeles, and I just HAD to get there. The magnet, of course, was Hollywood, especially The Palladium Ballroom, a huge gilded barn, but what a magnificent joint! Les Brown was the band I heard most often, and I could usually find a few girls willing to risk a dance with a lanky, pimply-faced kid.

But without a car, there was simply no way to GET to L.A.! So I bought a 1936 Plymouth sedan, the best set of wheels I could afford. The Base rule on cars was quite clear and was strictly enforced: NO cars on the Base unless they had passed a MECHANICAL INSPECTION and had been declared safe by the Base Motor Pool, with a *sticker* certifying that fact.

I was certain my old clunker would never pass, and I would consequently never make it to Hollywood and the Big Bands. So, using the mature judgment that had served me so well during the previous six years, I FORGED an inspection sticker! What chutzpah! I must say, however, that it must have been a convincing forgery. At least I was never caught, thank God!, even as the guards at the base gates leaned over to 'check' the sticker. If I HAD been caught, it would have meant court-martial and time in the Stockade; I had by now made it to Tech Sergeant, and I would lose my stripes in the bargain. Looking back on it, what a stupid chance to take! But whoever said teenagers have *ANY* kind of judgment…much less GOOD judgment?!

One of the most exciting moments occurred on Sunset Boulevard, not far from Hollywood and Vine. I was just ambling along enjoying the California weather and eyeing the California girls ['no harm in looking, just looking!'], when I was struck by a very unusual sound, one of the most beautiful sounds I had ever heard. I followed the music up to the second floor. There, in a large rehearsal studio, was an eight-piece marimba band…nothing but marimbas…HUGE bass marimbas vibrating with a deep jungle B O O M! baritones, tenors, altos, petite soprano marimbas. I've never encountered anything like it since. The band was playing beautifully…gorgeous harmony and rhythm. The tune was one we seldom hear today: the first line of the lyrics are, 'Spain, you're like a lady so fair, wearing a rose in her hair, there by the tropical sea.' Corny words, nice tune. The world would be a better place with more marimba bands!

Returning to the Base late at night, the road took me through miles of orange groves. In frosty weather, which was often, the smudge pots would be lit as farmers tried to ward off freezing and save their crop. If you mix the thick coastal fog of a California winter, with dense smoke from thousands of smudge pots, you get ZERO visibility. It's a wonder I was never killed!

It was late February 1949, and I was only six months away from discharge. I knew I had to go to college. I had to get an education, which was, hooray hooray!, already PAID FOR! But I simply could not go back to high school! That made no sense whatever to me. USAFI courses had convinced me there was no question but that I could handle college-level work. But how could I convince a university to *admit* me?

I decided to bracket the target, as the guys in artillery say. Based on my own hit-or-miss self-education up to this point, it seemed clear to me that if one was going to learn something, anything, you would ultimately learn it on your own…mainly by reading. The 'diploma,' the piece of paper at the end, was no more than a symbol, whose value was in direct proportion to the prestige attached to the school's name. Name-recognition was what mattered. Based on this line of thought, which I still think is not wrong, I applied to Oxford. They wrote back at once, quite politely saying I needed to 'know Latin and Greek.'

I then lowered my sights, and applied to the University of Kentucky. They wrote back after a long delay saying it was 'quite impossible to consider' an applicant who had never finished the tenth grade; I would have to 'return to Kentucky and finish high school.' *Same to you, Fella!*

I applied to Occidental College: it was in nearby Pasadena, which seemed appealing. I visited the campus and was impressed. But they turned me down flat: a simple 'NO.'

I then thought of Harvard, Yale, Princeton. Any hope, any hope at all, in that direction? After Oxford, it did NOT look promising. Still, they don't shoot you for TRYING! I didn't care for Yale, in the middle of what I imagined to be an ugly town. Harvard seemed too remote, too snooty, for a hillbilly. Okay, I'll try Princeton. The books say the campus is beautiful, and it's only fifty miles from New York, so maybe I could get in to hear some Big Band music.

Princeton was no more than a name to me. I had never been there, had never met anyone who had been there. But the name had prestige, and a piece of paper from that particular place struck me as worth more, or at least I thought it was, than one from the University of Kentucky, which didn't want me anyway!

Princeton's response gave me my *only hope.* The Dean of Admissions, Radcliffe Heermance, who had been there since he was a grad student and *preceptor* in 1909, replied with a letter that made sense. He said, 'Take the College Boards.' I did, with good results. I also sent transcripts of all of my USAFI work, solicited recommendations from my many—far TOO many!—high school teachers and principals, wrote to the Princeton Club of Louisville, and was interviewed by several alumni. I also wrote long letters to the Chairman of *every* Department, to *every* member of the Admissions Committee, and to *every* Member of the Princeton Board of Trustees.

It was overkill. But I HAD to make them understand that I HAD NEVER WANTED ANYTHING SO MUCH IN MY LIFE.

When I learned that I had been admitted, I realized that Princeton was taking a gamble...A BIG gamble! I resolved that this was one bet they...and I...would WIN! I would not blow my last, best chance.

But stupidity hangs in there, old habits die hard, and I nearly did!

Thus, in the last week of August 1949, an Air force friend discharged at March Air Force Base at the time same, joined up with me to share the driving and split expenses, as we set out in my dilapidated 1936 Plymouth. I hoped the car could make the trip, but I was not at all certain about this.

We took a meandering course...up Palomar Mountain to see the new Observatory, down to San Diego, then straight up the coast, Route 101, sightseeing at San Luis Obispo, San Juan Capistrano, and San Simeon. At Big Sur, the road degenerated to rough gravel; we drove late at night along some truly dangerous curves; one slip and you're over the cliff, into the Pacific. A doe and a baby fawn suddenly appeared in the headlights; the doe leaped clear, but the fawn was killed. I was heartbroken, and a little scared, since I had killed a deer in a State Park. We drove to the nearest Ranger Station, explained what had happened, and left the pitiful little carcass with the Rangers; I imagine this was a fairly common occurrence, and the Rangers had a little venison feast.

We continued to Carmel, San Francisco, across the Golden Gate Bridge, the Redwoods in John Muir Woods. We then turned east to Yosemite, where we spent a couple of days. The fastest, most direct route, one that promised even more spectacular scenery, was via Tuolumne; but Tioga Pass was almost 10,000 feet. My old clunker coughed and died, the victim of what other drivers called 'vapor lock.' The old Plymouth quit on a narrow stretch of mountain road, and cars were strung out for a mile behind us. Angry drivers helped us push the old crate to the side of the road. In time, the motor cooled, came to life again, and we soon made it over the crest: that ancient Plymouth moved much faster downhill.

Then an accident: we were descending a five-mile decline toward the flat 'Basin' of the Nevada desert. We had been eating lunch in the car, but the odor from a can of sardines, a Steinbeck memento bought at Cannery Row in Monterey, was annoying me. I was driving, and reached far out so as to heave the can well off the highway to the right.

Suddenly, we were off the road, speeding down a steep embankment, spinning around, out of control. We didn't flip, and the car came to rest in one piece, but completely turned around, facing uphill. We were unhurt, but very shaken up and scared.

I drove very carefully from then until five days later when I pulled into the quiet greenery of Lawerenceville, a famous prep school just down the road from Princeton. Of course I had to stop at The Jigger Shop, site of Hungry Smeed's pancake triumph, recounted in Owen Johnson's classic and very readable *Lawrenceville* series, which I had enjoyed years ago.

As I've gotten older, I've grown fond of the motto [did I invent it? I hope I did!] 'Constant Course Correction.' This mental metaphor conjures up an image of me as 'Captain' of my personal little boat, striving to reach some life goal. Like all of us, I'm buffeted by winds, strong currents push my boat this way and that, and the boat, with me in it!, is tossed about in rough seas. Events, contingencies, surprises, things no one can anticipate or control, really can, and probably will, throw you and me…all of us…far off-course.

But I believe, or at least I HOPE!, that if one has a clear goal…a goal you *really* want to reach…and if you are alert, and keep your hand on the tiller at all times, and are prepared, and are willing to alter direction and steer a new course…in short, if one perseveres (like The Hunter, The Settler, The Miller, The Sawyer, all 'bound and determined!') and constantly correct our course, isn't there a fair chance…we can maybe find our way…get back on course, get to where we want to go? Who knows?, maybe we really will reach some worthwhile, achievable goal?

For far too many decades I was just a passenger, not really steering my boat, mainly just along for the ride. This attitude, and many other bad habits, got me into trouble, and I am not happy remembering that.

But I have been blessed beyond all deserving. Call it the grace of God (though as a Secular Humanist, I suppose I have no right to use the name of God). For me, getting my little boat back on course happened…thanks to the never-failing love of my wife, and the support of two strong sons, plus plenty of luck…and the kindness of strangers: people like Ada Dozier Cooke and Flo Bratten. If you have read this far, I suspect you'll agree that a stubborn young nitwit like me certainly needed LOTS of luck! Principal Danowski was right.

Memories of Princeton, of the Foreign Service, my twelve years as administrator of scientific studies of greenhouse climate change, my foray into the history of Kentucky exploration, and my years as a singer and bandleader, must wait, as Paul Harvey says…'The Rest of The Story.' I hope to live long enough to write those stories. Maybe you will want to read them! I hope so! If you do, may I Thank You *now*, in advance.

0-595-21175-5

Made in the USA
Lexington, KY
23 June 2013